GET YOUR
BUNS
IN HERE

Laurel A. Wicks

Recipes for mouthwatering buns, cookies,
pastries, brownies, breads, rolls, candies,
pies, tarts, muffins, and other baked delights.

TEN SPEED PRESS

1☯ **TEN SPEED PRESS**
P.O. Box 7123
Berkeley, California 94707

Book Design by Fifth Street Design
Cover Design by Fifth Street Design
Typography by Ann Flanagan Typography
Ilustrations by Stuart Auld

Library of Congress Cataloging-in-Publication Data

Wicks, Laurel A.
  Get your buns in here.
  Includes index.
  1. Baking.   I. Title.
TX763.W47 1987   641.7′1   82-90437
ISBN 0-89815-192-9

Printed in the United States of America

  2 3 4 5 — 91 90 89

Acknowledgments

There are many people to thank for this endeavor, beginning with my parents, whose lives reflect a vision and support that does not fail me. The generosity and encouragement of John Nooney, Alfred Ford, Ron Shapiro, and Felix Buchenroth, Jr. made the project possible. Blanche was my left hand person. Her name has been too long missing. The graphics are the product of Stuart Auld's creative mind. Diane Kaup Benefiel and Marie Case guided the layout and assembly of the first printing. Without the help of Maurice, it's hard to tell what might have been. Individual creations were developed from the inspirations of the people given credit at the top of recipes. Employees, family, neighbors, customers, and students make up the fibers of my life and business. The dividing line between those two categories may become subtle or fade away entirely. Together they have woven the fabric of an entity known as Bru's Buns & Breads.

To My Mother,
who presented me with a choice
when I was little,
"Would you like to weed the flower garden,
or make some cookies?"

Table of Contents

INTRODUCTION   vii

NOTES ON THE RECIPES   viii

NOTES ON HIGH ALTITUDE BAKING   ix

CHAPTER 1 ■ BREAKFAST

As the Sheep...   3
Buttermilk Coffeecake   4
Braided Cardamom Buns   5
Danish Pastry   6
Granola   8

Hot Crossed Buns   9
Sweet E. Buns   10
Raisin Brioche Ring   11
Poppy Seed Rolls   12

CHAPTER 2 ■ COOKIES

Almond   14
Chewy Oatmeal   15
Chocolate Chip   16
Chocolate Peanut Butter
    Pinwheels   17
Cut Out   18
Ginger Crinkles   19
Half Moons / Sour Cream   20
Orange   21

Pecan Nougats   22
Peanut Butter   23
Refrigerator   24
Scottish Shortbread   25
Sesame   26
Shelly's Chocolate Fantasies   27
Snickerdoodles   28
Soft Molasses   29
Thumbprints   30

CHAPTER 3 ■ DESSERTS & PASTRIES

Baklava   32
Blue Cheese Cake with Grape
    Sauce   34
Bread Pudding with Rum Sauce   35
Cannolis   36
Chocolate Eclairs   38

Chocolate Soufflé   39
Linzertorte   40
Lemon Sponge Pudding   41
Too Chocolate Chocolate   42
Cheesecake Brujaja   43
Scones   44

CHAPTER 4 ■ SQUARES & BARS

Birdfood Bars   46
Brownies   47
Butterscotch Squares   48
Cream Cheese Brownies   49

Chewy Peanut Fingers   50
Date Bars   50
Healthy Fingers   51
Lebkuchen   52

CHAPTER 5 ■ SWEET BREADS

Apple Nut   54
Apricot   55
Banana Nut   56
Boston Brown   57
Coconut   58
Cranberry   59

Date Nut   60
Irish Soda   61
Lemon Pecan   62
Pumpkin   63
Zucchini   64

CHAPTER 6 ▪ BREADS & ROLLS

The Wheats   67
Beer Bread   68
Cardamom Rolls   69
Cheese Bread   70
Dark Rye   72
English Muffins   73
Egg Bagels   74
French Loaves   76

Logan Bread   77
Light Rye   78
Oatmeal Sunflower Millet Bread   80
Whole Wheat Bread   81
Onion Rolls   82
Ragbrod   84
Spinach Loaf   85
Tortillas   86

CHAPTER 7 ▪ SOURDOUGH

Sourdough Starter   88
Sourdough French Bread   90

Sourdough Rye Bread   91

CHAPTER 8 ▪ CANDY

Divinity   94
English Toffee   95

Sesame Crunch   96
Penuche   96

CHAPTER 9 ▪ CAKES & MUFFINS

Banana   98
Basic Yellow   99
Black Forest   100
Blueberry Bran Muffins   101
Carrot   102
Corn Muffins, Cajun Style   103
Devil's Food   104
Ebony   105
Fairport Orange   106
German Chocolate   107

Hundred Dollar   108
Orange   109
Poppy Seed   110
Pumpkin   111
Sour Cream Pound   112
Strawberry Muffins   113
Sweet Potato Muffins   114
Upside Down   115
White Chocolate   116

CHAPTER 10 ▪ PIES & TARTS

Basic Pastry   118
Armadillos' Ecstasies   119
Banana Cream   120
Chocolate Pecan Bourbon   121
Buttermilk Custard   122
Chocolate Cream Tarts   122
Cranberry Apple   123
Key Lime   124

Lemon Meringue   125
Peach Daiquiri   126
Peanut Butter   127
Pecan   128
Strawberry Rhubarb Tarts   128
Pumpkin   129
Sweet Potato   130

CHAPTER 11 ▪ FROSTINGS, GLAZES, & ICINGS

Mocha Butter Cream   132
Orange Frosting   132
Raspberry Icing   132
Sweet Bread Glaze I   132
Sweet Bread Glaze II   133
Sweet E. Bun Glaze   133

Chocolate Glaze   133
Chocolate Frosting   133
Brandy Orange Icing   134
Cream Cheese Icing   134
Danish Glaze   134
Lebkuchen Glaze   134

Introduction

In the fall of 1974 a project began which has consumed my life for many years. It began as a dream. It molded itself into a reality. A tiny log cabin in Jackson, Wyoming, originally built as a blacksmith shop, was transformed into a bakery. With borrowed money and some antique equipment local legend was born: Bru's Buns & Breads. This book contains most of the recipes and a few of the memories from that establishment.

The plan was to show the world that healthy foods were the ticket to happiness. My background in business was non-existent. A few home-sized recipes, all made with honey were the beginning. From these evolved major changes in style. The first customers were welcomed on St. Patrick's Day, 1975. "We want brownies, chocolate brownies!" "Cookies!" "Make us candy!" resounded the requests. The shock registered heavily. These people didn't want to hear my rap on health, and keeping the fans happy was a necessity. Since that day, there have been changes.

My product line has been tempered for social compatibility and economic survival. I have learned to use white sugar as well as honey. I can cook for macrobiotics and omnivores, over campfires or in restaurants. My philosophy remains essentially the same. Eating is a vital part of our lives each day. The quality of the ingredients determines the outcome of the product. The foods that we consume literally become us. The materials our bodies and brains use to create are limited to what we feed ourselves. Bru's Buns & Breads always used the finest quality ingredients: real chocolate, extracts (rather than flavorings), butter, safflower or soy oils, unbleached flour, whole grains, fresh fruits. I suggest that you do the same.

The recipes in this book are a framework from which to learn. Experiment! Sometimes I make these recipes just as they are written. Often I make substitutions. I leave out the nuts so I may share a treat with my brother who doesn't like nuts. The original recipe should be nutritious. Perhaps, in the process of making something, I discover that there are no lemons in the house. Be flexible. It helps.

Weather and mood affect baking. Low cloud ceilings slow down the rising process. Angry people's cakes fall. It helps to be sensitive to the prevailing conditions. Baking is an excellent form of therapy. The creative process can be an extremely pleasurable experience!

This book is for you. Have fun. Be tempted and create temptations. May the buns always rise.

Notes on the Recipes

Following are some explanations to aid your baking adventures with this book.

- Read the whole recipe before you begin cooking.
- Note the yield stated at the top of the recipe.
- The oven temperature is also given at the top of each recipe. "Preheat to" means that the recipe does not take long to mix, so you should be sure to have the oven ready. "Bake at" means that the procedure takes longer, so there will be time for the oven to reach the right temperature while you are assembling the dish.
- Some recipes suggest preparation of certain portions in a specific order. Timing is important. Some things are highly perishable during mixing.
- It helps to prepare baking pans before you start to mix.

- Parchment paper is great for lining cake pans or for baking cookies or brownies. It keeps food from being too oily and makes the pans extremely easy to clean.
- Grease pans with vegetable oil rather than butter, which burns easily.
- I don't recommend aluminum mixing containers. They react chemically with eggs, citrus, and many other substances, including your body.
- To create a buttermilk or sour milk substitute, add a teaspoon of vinegar to one cup sweet milk and wait a few moments.
- Salt is a flavor enhancer. It may be eliminated for health or dietary reasons. Salt retards the growth of yeast.
- "c" stands for cup
- "T" stands for tablespoon
- "t" stands for teaspooon
- Some items, especially cookies and squares, continue to bake for a few moments after coming from the oven. Don't let them over-bake.
- To test cakes or sweet breads, insert a clean toothpick vertically in the center of the pan. If the cake is done, the toothpick will be clean when removed.
- Brown paper is useful for cooling some items. It also catches drips of glazes which tend to seize up like mortar on shelves and floors.

Notes on High Altitude Baking

These recipes were developed in Jackson Hole, Wyoming, at an altitude of 6,200 feet. It is my opinion that much of what one reads about high altitude baking is intimidating hype. Different conditions do exist at different altitudes, but the patterns are entirely logical.

At high altitudes there is less atmosphere above you; there is less force pushing down. Therefore, cakes and breads rise more easily. This means that less leavening is needed. So decrease slightly the amount of yeast, baking soda, baking powder, or sourdough starter.

At high altitudes liquids also boil at a much lower temperature, a phenomenon that affects baking. For each 1,000 feet above sea level, it is necessary to decrease the sweetener by one tablespoon per cup, and to increase the flour by the same amount.

Because the air is less dense at high altitudes, it doesn't hold heat as well. It takes a bit more time to bake at high altitudes. Check your oven often to make sure your buns don't burn.

Conversely, if you are baking at, or below (don't laugh), sea level, or if there is a heavy cloud cover, you should reverse the modifications, i.e., increase the leavening and sweetining, decrease the flour, and bake for a shorter time.

Doesn't all that sound easy? It is. Baking isn't a one shot deal, it's an evolution. If you try a recipe and consider the results acceptable, but a little less than perfect, make some notes for yourself on the page as you proceed. Modify. Believe in yourself. Try. Be creative.

If you have questions, write them down, and send them in my direction:
Bru's Buns
Box 1470
Jackson, Wyoming 83001

BREAKFAST

As the Sheep Attack the Bakery Screaming Nonsense

S. Doug Hettinger

Having sharpened the knife for the seventeenth
    time,
I see I've committed a sweetie bun crime.
In an effort to capture an absolute fluff
Was the tray barely pulled from the heat
    soon enough.
With all of my knowledge summoned up for
    this try
What have I created: breakfast rolls, slightly dry.
Hopefully passing for a bit overdone,
They won't sit on the shelf being buncumbersome.
As I lesson-learned homeward the walk slowly trod,
Will I welcome my bed and the land ruled by Nod.

Good-morning, bru.

Buttermilk Coffeecake

Russell Gilliam

Preheat oven to 350°
Makes 1 9" ring

1½ c unbleached
  flour
⅓ c granulated sugar
½ c brown sugar
½ t ground ginger
1 t cinnamon
⅜ c softened butter
1 egg
⅔ c buttermilk
½ t baking soda
½ baking powder
½ t salt

½ c pecan pieces
2 t cinnamon

Measure into a bowl the flour, sugars, ginger, cinnamon, and salt. Stir until thoroughly mixed. Measure in the butter and cut in with a fork or a pastry blender.

Remove ⅔ cup of this mixture from the bowl. Add this to a small bowl which contains the pecans and the 2 t of cinnamon. Stir and set aside.

Beat the egg into the batter, then gradually add the buttermilk. At this point it is extremely important to whip the batter until it is light and smooth.

Stir into the batter the baking soda and baking powder. After these have been well stirred, pour the batter into a pan which has been oiled and lined with paper. Spread the batter evenly. Cover the top with the crumb mixture.

Place the coffee cake in an oven preheated to 350°. Baking time is approximately 25 minutes. I find this cake to be quite delicate during the baking process. It will fall if disturbed. Allow to cool 5 minutes before removing from pan.

Braided Cardamom Buns

Bake at 350°
Makes about 2 dozen

1½ c warm water
½ c vegetable oil
½ c honey
2½ T yeast
2 eggs
1 T ground cardamom
1 t salt
½ c powdered milk
6 c unbleached flour

milk
granulated sugar

In a large bowl combine the water, oil, and honey. Stir until the honey is mixed. Sprinkle in the yeast and stir until dissolved. When the yeast rises to the surface and begins to foam, add the eggs, cardamom, powdered milk, and ½ the flour. Beat well. Allow to rest for 10 minutes. Add the salt and the remaining flour.

Turn the dough onto a slightly floured surface, and knead about 5 minutes. Return to the bowl, and after oiling the dough lightly, cover, and allow to rise until doubled.

Punch down and knead. Divide into 2 dozen pieces. Roll each into a coil about 7" long. Form each into a knot. Tuck both ends under the roll. Place on an oiled baking tray.

Brush the rolls with milk and sprinkle with sugar. Allow to rise until doubled before placing in the oven. At this time preheat the oven to 350°. Bake until browned, approximately 35 minutes. Remove from the trays and cool on a wire rack.

Danish Pastry

Bake at 400°
Makes about 4 dozen

8 c unbleached flour
½ c granulated sugar
4 eggs at room
  temperature
1½ c milk
½ c hot water
4 T yeast

1¼ lb. butter
cinnamon
granulated sugar
butter

Mix the flour and sugar in a large mixing bowl. Break the eggs into a small bowl or cup. In a measuring cup, combine the milk, water, and the yeast. Stir the yeast constantly until it dissolves, but is not foamy. It is very important that the yeast does not begin to work. Pour the liquids into the dry mixture. Stir in slightly. Add the eggs and mix until kneadable. Turn onto a board, and knead until the texture becomes smooth, and the dough is quite glossy. This takes almost forever.

Let the dough rest for at least 10 minutes in the refrigerator, well wrapped. Roll the dough into a rectangle slightly less than ½ inch thick. Spread ⅔ of this rectangle with butter which is firm, but not hard. Fold the unbuttered portion of this rectangle toward the center, then the other end over this to create 5 layers (dough / butter / dough / butter / dough). Roll out again to the same size and repeat the procedure. All of the butter should be used by the third repetition.

Temperature is an extremely important consideration. This dough must remain cool enough to prevent the yeast from working and the butter from melting. Be sure to return the dough to the refrigerator any time it becomes too warm. If well-wrapped it may remain refrigerated for hours.

The rolling and folding process should be repeated 3 more times. The last fold will be difficult. When the dough is rolled to the large rectangular shape, spread the whole surface with a thin layer of softened butter. Then cover ½ the dough with a mixture of equal portions of cinnamon and sugar. Fold in ½ and return to the refrigerator until the butter is hard.

Roll the dough one last time into a rectangle ½ inch thick. Cut into strips ½ inch wide, a few at a time. Holding one end of a strip, roll the other with your hand until the whole length is an even spiral. Curl this spiral into a flat coil. Tuck the end under. Place on an oiled and floured tray.

Allow to rise in a cool place. Slow rising is important to prevent cracking and to prevent the butter layers from melting. When doubled, preheat the oven to 400°. Gently press a thumb into the center of each pastry, and fill with preserves just before baking. Remove from oven when golden and glaze while warm, but not hot.

Granola

Preheat oven to 325°
Makes about 8 cups

4 c rolled oats
$\frac{2}{3}$ c sunflower seeds
$\frac{1}{3}$ c sesame seeds
$\frac{2}{3}$ c cashews
$\frac{2}{3}$ c almonds
$\frac{2}{3}$ c walnuts
1 c coconut
$\frac{1}{2}$ c vegetable oil
$\frac{2}{3}$ c honey
2 T vanilla extract
$\frac{1}{2}$ t salt
$\frac{1}{3}$ t ground cloves
$\frac{2}{3}$ t cinnamon

In a small saucepan combine the liquids and the spices. Heat, stirring occasionally to prevent burning. Do not allow to boil.

While the syrup is heating, mix the dry ingredients in a large bowl. Pour the sauce over the dry mixture while stirring.

Spread on oiled trays and place in oven. Bake 20 minutes or until golden, stirring occasionally to insure even browning.

Optional raisins, dates, or other fruits may be added to the mix after it is cooled.

Hot Crossed Buns

Bake at 350°
Makes 2 dozen

2½ c hot water
¼ c butter, softened
2½ T yeast
⅔ c honey
2 eggs

1 c raisins
1½ t cinnamon
½ t ground cloves
½ t nutmeg
2 oranges (juice and grated peel)
1 c powdered milk
1 t salt
8 c unbleached flour

GLAZE:
1 T water
1½ T lemon juice
2 c powdered sugar

Break the eggs into a tiny bowl. Add the orange juice and grated peel and set aside. Combine the hot water, honey, and the softened butter in a mixing bowl and stir until the butter is melted. Gradually stir in the yeast and stir until dissolved. Allow to rest until the yeast begins to foam.

Add half the flour and beat at least 100 strokes. Let rise for 10 minutes. Add the spices, egg mix, powdered milk, salt, raisins, and a little more flour. Stir until evenly mixed. Gradually add more flour until a soft dough is formed. Knead on a lightly floured board for about 5 minutes. Shape into a ball. Lightly oil the surface. Return to bowl. Cover and allow to rise until doubled.

Punch down the dough and knead. Let the dough rest while making an egg wash from the white of an egg and 1 Tablespoon of water. Oil baking sheets.

Shape the dough into balls about 1½ inches. Place on baking sheets and brush with the egg wash.

Let rise until almost doubled and bake until golden, about 20 minutes.

Glaze with crosses while slightly warm.

Sweet E. Buns

The originals from
Barbara Sanford Smith

Bake at 325°
Makes 2 bun rings

2 c milk
¼ c honey
¼ c butter
2 T yeast
1 t salt
4½ c unbleached
   flour

melted butter
brown sugar
cinnamon
fruits & nuts

Warm the milk and honey. Pour into a mixing bowl and stir in the yeast until dissolved. When the yeast rises to the surface and becomes foamy, pour in the butter and approximately 2 cups of flour. Beat until smooth and shiny. Allow the batter to rise for 10 minutes. Add the salt and another cup of flour. Stir until smooth. Gradually add more flour. This dough should remain too sticky to handle without counter and hands being well floured.

Allow to rise again for 10 to 15 minutes. While the dough is rising, prepare the chopped fruits and nuts of your choice to be the filling. Oil and flour tube pans or trays.

Punch down the dough, then turn it onto a well floured counter and roll into a rectangle about ¼″ thick. Using a pastry brush, cover the rectangle with melted butter. Spread this with brown sugar, then sprinkle with cinnamon (and a trace of nutmeg or cloves). Spread the fruits and nuts evenly over the dough. Roll the dough, and cut into 1″ slices. Arrange these in the prepared pans, touching but not too crowded to allow room to grow. Set aside in a draftless place.

Preheat oven. When the buns have almost doubled, place in the oven. Allow to bake until golden on the outside, about 30 minutes. The buns should spring back in the center after a light touch.

The buns should cool for a few minutes before being removed from pans. They should be glazed while still warm.

Raisin Brioche Ring

Rebecca Silva Stansberry

Bake at 350°
Makes 2 rings

½ c water
1 c scalded milk
⅓ c honey
¼ c butter
2 T yeast
1½ c raisins
3 eggs
1 t salt
5½ c unbleached
   flour

1 egg yolk

Cover the raisins with hot water. In a large bowl combine the scalded milk, water, honey, and butter. Stir until the honey is dissolved and the butter melted. Sprinkle in the yeast while stirring. Let rest until it begins to foam. Add the raisins, well drained, and the eggs. Stir in 3 cups of flour and beat well. Let rest for 10 minutes.

Add the salt and the rest of the flour. Turn this soft dough onto a lightly floured surface and knead for 5 minutes. Place in a greased bowl, turning to grease the surface. Cover and allow to rise until doubled.

Punch down the dough and knead lightly. Divide the dough in ½ and allow to rest for 10 minutes. Oil and flour two 9" baking pans with sides 1½" to 2". Shape each ½ of the dough into 8 balls and place in the pans with a little space between each, and the sides of the pan. With pastry scissors or a serrated knife slash X's on each dough ball. Allow to rise until doubled.

Bake about 25 minutes. Remove from the oven and brush surfaces with an egg yolk beaten with 1 T water. Return to the oven and bake until golden.

Remove from pans while hot, and cool on wire racks.

Poppy Seed Rolls

Rebecca Silva Stansberry

Bake at 350°
Makes 2 rolls

2 T active dry yeast
5 to 6 c unbleached
  flour
1½ c milk
⅓ c granulated sugar
⅓ c vegetable oil
1 t salt
3 eggs

¾ c poppy seeds
⅓ c honey
½ c chopped nuts
1 T grated lemon peel
1 stiffly beaten egg
  white

In a large mixing bowl, combine the yeast with 2 cups of sifted flour. Combine the milk, sugar, vegetable oil and salt and heat until warm, but not hot. Stir to prevent scorching. Add this to the dry ingredients. Add the eggs. Beat until smooth, about 3 to 5 minutes. Add enough flour to make a moderately stiff dough. Turn onto a lightly floured surface and knead until smooth and satiny, about 5 to 10 minutes. Shape into a ball. Put in a lightly greased bowl, turning once to grease the surface. Cover and let rise in a warm place until double, about an hour.

Meanwhile make poppy seed filling: Pour 1 cup of boiling water over the poppy seeds. Let stand for 30 minutes. Drain thoroughly. Grind the poppy seeds in a blender. Stir in the nuts, honey, and lemon peel. Fold in the egg white.

Punch down the dough. Divide the dough into halves. Cover and let rise for 10 minutes. On a lightly floured board, roll one part of the dough into a rectangle 20"x8". Spread half the filling evenly over the dough. Roll up and seal the ends. Place seam side down in a 9"x3"x5" loaf pan, well greased. Repeat. Let rise until double, about 45 minutes. Bake for 35–40 minutes.

COOKIES

Almond Cookies

Preheat oven to 300°
Makes 3 dozen

1¼ c granulated sugar
1¼ c butter
2 eggs
1 t almond extract
½ t lemon extract
½ t salt
1 t baking powder
3 c unbleached flour
36 whole almonds

Thoroughly cream the butter and sugar. Add the eggs and beat until light in color and texture. While stirring, add the lemon extract, almond extract, and salt. Add the baking powder with the first cup of flour. Gradually add the rest of the flour, mixing thoroughly until the dough is firm, but not dry. Shape into 1" balls, place on an unoiled baking sheet, flatten, and press an almond into the center of each.

Bake for 15 to 20 minutes. Allow 5 minutes cooling time before removing from trays.

Chewy Oatmeal Cookies

Preheat oven to 350°
Makes 6 dozen

1¼ c butter
1 c brown sugar
1 c granulated sugar
2 eggs
1 t vanilla extract
½ t salt
1 t nutmeg
1 c coconut
2½ c rolled oats
1 t baking soda
1¼ c unbleached flour

Thoroughly cream the butter and sugars. Whip in the eggs until light. Add the vanilla, salt and nutmeg and stir. Add the coconut and the oats, and blend. Let the dough rest a few minutes before adding the flour. This will allow the coconut and the oats to absorb a bit of moisture. Add the baking soda, and gradually incorporate the flour into the mixture. The dough should be a little sticky, but not runny.

Roll into 1" balls and bake on a lightly oiled sheet. Bake until lightly golden, which takes about 15 minutes.

Chocolate Chip Cookies

Preheat oven to 350°
Makes 5 dozen

1½ c butter
1⅛ c granulated sugar
3 eggs
1½ t baking soda
1 t salt
1½ t vanilla extract
3⅜ c unbleached
 flour
12 ounces chocolate
 chips

Thoroughly cream the butter and sugars. Add the eggs and whip until light. Mix in the baking soda, salt, and vanilla. Add flour, stirring occasionally. The dough will be quite sticky. Stir in the chocolate chips.

Flour hands while working with this dough to keep it from sticking. Roll in 1" balls. Place on a lightly oiled baking sheet, and bake until golden, about 12 minutes. To make sure these cookies remain chewy, take them from the oven before they are done in the center, and store them in an airtight container as soon as they are cool.

Chocolate Peanut Butter Pinwheels

Mom

Preheat oven to 350°
Makes about 3 dozen

1 c butter
2 c granulated sugar
1 c peanut butter
2 eggs
4 T milk
2½ c unbleached flour
1 t baking soda
¼ t salt
2 c chocolate chips, melted

Cream the butter and sugar. Add peanut butter, eggs, and milk. Stir until blended. Add the flour, soda, and salt and stir until thoroughly mixed. Divide the dough in half.

On a lightly floured board or wax paper roll out each half into a rectangle 15"x8"x¼". Spread the melted chocolate evenly over the dough. Roll up to form logs 15" long and about 2" in diameter. Wrap tightly.

Refrigerate for 20 to 30 minutes. Slice roll into cookies ¼" thick. Bake on an ungreased cookie sheet for 8 to 10 minutes. Yummo! The best in years.

Cut Out Cookies

Preheat oven to 325°
Makes 3 dozen

1 c butter
1 c granulated sugar
2 eggs
1 t baking soda
2 t cream of tartar
½ t salt
1 t vanilla extract
3 c unbleached
  flour

Thoroughly cream the butter and sugar. Add the eggs and whip until light. Stir in the vanilla. Sift the flour, then add to it the baking soda, cream of tartar and salt. Sift the flour into the batter gradually, blending it in. The dough will be sticky. Cover and refrigerate for at least 2 hours.

Roll on a well-floured surface, with additonal flour on top of the dough to prevent sticking to the rolling pin. It also helps to dip the cookie cutters in flour to prevent sticking. Transfer the cookies to lightly oiled trays. Bake until golden, about 10 minutes.

Frost only after thoroughly cooled.

Ginger Crinkles

Janet McPherson Wershow

Preheat oven to 350°
Makes 6 dozen

1⅓ c butter
2 c granulated sugar
2 eggs
½ c molasses
1 T baking soda
1 t salt
2 t cinnamon
1 t cloves
2 t ginger
4½ c unbleached
  flour

Thoroughly cream the butter and sugar. Add the eggs and whip until light. Add the molasses, stir in, and add the baking soda, salt, cinnamon, cloves, and ginger. After the spices are blended into the mixture, gradually add the flour. Shape the cookies into 1" balls. Roll in granulated sugar. Bake on lightly oiled trays for 12 minutes.

Half Moons Sour Cream Cookies

Catherine Newman Donaldson

Preheat oven to 375°
Makes about 3 dozen

2 eggs
1 c granulated sugar
½ c sour cream
⅓ c butter
2 c unbleached
   flour
½ t baking soda

Thoroughly beat the eggs. Add the sugar, sour cream, and butter. Whip until light. Add the flour and baking soda and stir until smooth. Drop by the tablespoon onto an oiled, floured sheet. Bake until they spring back. Make sure they do not brown.

To create Half Moons: After the cookies are cooled, frost ½ the bottom of each cookie with chocolate frosting and the other ½ with white.

The alternate solution, and my Grandma's favorite was to add 1 t nutmeg to the batter, turn the batter onto a well floured board, roll out to ⅜" and cut with a scallop-edged cookie cutter. Transfer the cookies to baking sheets. Sprinkle with granulated sugar, and press raisins into the centers before baking.

Orange Cookies

David Samuelson's Aunt Edith

Preheat oven to 350°
Makes about 5 dozen

1½ c granulated sugar
1 c butter
3 eggs
1 t salt
1 c sour cream
1 t baking soda
1 t baking powder
3¾ c flour
juice and grated rind
  of 1 orange

Cream the butter and sugar thoroughly. Add the eggs and whip until light. Add the salt, sour cream, and the orange juice and rind. Also add 1 cup of flour and stir. Add the baking soda and powder with the next cup of flour. Gradually stir in all of the flour. The batter will be quite moist.

Drop by the tablespoon onto an oiled and slightly floured sheet. Bake until the cookies spring back from a light touch, which is before they brown, approximately 10 minutes.

When cool, frost the bottom side with Orange Frosting.

Pecan Nougats

Mom

Preheat oven to 350°
Makes about 3 dozen

½ c butter
2 T granulated sugar
¼ t vanilla extract
⅞ c unbleached flour
¼ t salt
1 c finely chopped
  pecans

powdered sugar

Thoroughly cream the butter and sugar. Add the vanilla and blend in. In a separate container mix the flour, nuts, and salt. Gradually incorporate this mix into a smooth dough.

Shape into 1″ balls. Place on lightly oiled cookie sheets and bake about 10 to 12 minutes.

Roll the cookies in powdered sugar while they are still hot and again after they have cooled.

Peanut Butter Cookies

Preheat oven to 350°
Makes about 4 dozen

⅔ c butter
1 c peanut butter
1 c granulated sugar
1¼ c brown sugar
3 eggs
1 t vanilla extract
½ t salt
1½ t baking powder
1 t baking soda
2¾ c unbleached
   flour

Cream together the butter and the peanut butter. Beat in both kinds of sugar until smooth. Add the eggs and beat until the texture and color become noticeably lighter. Stir in the vanilla, salt, and rising agents. Gradually add flour, stirring until well blended. This dough should not be too dry when complete.

Shape into balls and flatten with a fork to form perpendicular stripes. Bake on lightly oiled sheets until golden.

Refrigerator Cookies

Mom

Bake at 400°
Makes 4 dozen

½ c butter
2 eggs
1 c brown sugar
½ t salt
½ t cream of tartar
½ t baking soda
1 t vanilla extract
¾ c chopped pecans
2 c unbleached flour

This recipe should be prefaced by saying that the real secret ingredient is wild hickory nuts. I wish you the best of luck finding them.

Cream the butter and brown sugar thoroughly. Add the eggs and beat until light in color and texture. Blend in the salt, cream of tartar, baking soda, and vanilla. Stir in the pecans. Gradually mix in the flour.

Shape into rolls, wrap in waxed paper, and refrigerate until completely chilled.

Preheat the oven to 400°. Slice the rolls ⅜" thick and place on a lightly oiled baking sheet. Bake until light brown.

Scottish Shortbread

Shena's Granny

Preheat oven to 325°
Makes about 3 dozen

1 c butter
¾ c granulated sugar
2¼ c unbleached
  flour

Thoroughly cream the butter and sugar. The butter should be soft but not at all liquid. Stir in the flour. Knead the dough for about 15 minutes. This is an important step to prevent toughness.

Roll the dough on a floured counter until it is ⅜" thick. Cut into fingers, rectangular shapes about ¾" by 3". Place on a lightly oiled tray. Make a pattern of holes on each shortbread with a fork. Sprinkle with granulated sugar. Bake until golden, about 15 minutes.

Sesame Cookies

Preheat oven to 350°
Makes 4 dozen

¾ c butter
1 c brown sugar
1 egg
1 t vanilla extract
½ t baking soda
1 t baking powder
½ t salt
½ c coconut
1 c sesame seeds
2 c unbleached flour

Roast the sesame seeds and the coconut on a clean tray until golden, stirring occasionally. Thoroughly cream the butter and the brown sugar. Add the egg and beat until light. Add the vanilla, salt, baking soda, and baking powder. Stir. Blend in the sesame seeds and coconut. Gradually add the flour until the mix is moist, but not sticky. Roll into 1" balls and bake on an oiled sheet, about 12 minutes, or until golden.

Shelly's Chocolate Fantasies

Preheat oven to 350°
Makes 6 dozen

1¼ c butter
1½ c granulated sugar
1¾ c brown sugar
3 eggs
½ t salt
2 t baking soda
1 c cocoa
1 c walnuts
2 t vanilla extract
3¾ c unbleached
  flour

Thoroughly cream the butter and the sugars. Add the eggs and beat until light in color and texture, at least 5 minutes. Next, add salt, cocoa, walnuts, and vanilla, and stir. Measure in the baking soda, and gradually add the flour until the dough is moist, but not sticky.

Shape into 1" balls. Roll these in powdered sugar, and press onto a lightly oiled baking sheet. Bake for about 12 minutes. It is important to remove them from the oven before they become hard or dry.

Snickerdoodles

(The cookies that make you laugh)
Catherine Newman Donaldson

Bake at 400°
Makes about 4 dozen

1 c butter
2 eggs
1½ c granulated sugar
2 t cream of tartar
1 t baking soda
¼ t salt
2⅔ c unbleached flour
½ c raisins

cinnamon
granulated sugar

Thoroughly cream the butter and sugar. Add the eggs and beat until smooth and light. Measure into this mixture the cream of tartar, salt, and baking soda. Stir into batter. Gradually add the flour and stir until evenly mixed. Add the raisins, being sure they are evenly distributed.

Shape into balls almost 1" in diameter. Roll these in a bowl of cinnamon and white sugar of equal portions.

Press onto an ungreased baking sheet, and bake until they start to brown.

Soft Molasses Cookies

Grandma Jones

Preheat oven to 350°
Makes about 3 dozen

¾ c butter

¼ c brown sugar

½ c molasses

½ c buttermilk

¼ t salt

½ t cinnamon

1 t baking soda

1¾ c unbleached
   flour

Combine the softened butter and the brown sugar. Mix until smooth. Add the molasses and mix until smooth. Stir in the buttermilk until the mixture is evenly blended.

Mix the salt, cinnamon, and baking soda into the flour, then gradually mix these dry ingredients into the wet mixture.

Drop from a greased tablespoon onto an oiled cookie sheet. They are done when they bounce back from a soft-fingered touch.

Thumbprints

Mom

Preheat oven to 350°
Makes about 3 dozen

1 c butter
½ c granulated sugar
3 egg yolks
1 t vanilla extract
2 c unbleached flour
½ t salt

about 3 dozen nuts
or candies, or about
¼ cup preserves

Thoroughly cream the butter and sugar. Stir in the egg yolks one at a time, then add the vanilla and thoroughly beat again. Blend in the flour and salt. Cover and refrigerate for 1 hour.

Roll into 1″ balls. Place these on a lightly oiled cookie sheet. Make a thumbprint depression in the top of each cookie. Fill with a nut or candy or preserves.

Bake for about 10 minutes or until lightly golden.

DESSERTS & PASTRIES

Baklava

Preheat oven to 300°
Makes 1 pan 9"x13"

1 lb. phyllo
¾ lb. butter
3 c finely chopped
  nuts

SYRUP:
3 c water
2½ c honey
1 T lemon juice
1 t finely grated
  lemon peel
6 whole cloves
1 stick cinnamon
1 star anise

Melt the butter, and after letting it sit undisturbed for a few moments, clarify it by skimming the foam from the surface. Then separate the clear yellow liquid from the milky white liquid in the bottom. Discard all but the pure butter.

Using a pastry brush, cover the bottom and sides of a baking dish 9"x13"x2" with a thin layer of butter. Open the phyllo and place one leaf of this paper thin pastry in the bottom of the pan. Butter the top. Add another sheet of phyllo, then butter, until ¼ of the phyllo leaves have been used. Spread 1 c of the nuts evenly over the surface. Continue with the phyllo, butter repetition until ½ is incorporated, at which point another layer of nuts should be added. This continues until all of the phyllo and nuts are used. Using a very sharp knife, cut the baklava into diamond shaped pieces.

Concerning the nuts: Tradition dictates the use of walnuts. I have used a mixture of nuts. My favorite combination is 1 c cashews, 1 c almonds, and 1 c pecans. Please yourself.

Place the pan in the oven and turn down the heat to 250°. Baking time is approximately 2 hours. The baklava will rise and the layers will separate. It should be light and golden when done.

In a saucepan combine all the ingredients of the syrup. Again, tradition says to use sugar instead of honey. You may, if you wish. Bring the syrup to a boil while stirring. Reduce the heat immediately and simmer until the proper consistency is reached. This should be done while the pastry is in the oven. Remove the spices.

Take the baklava from the oven and slowly pour ½ the sauce over it. Return to the oven for 10 minutes. Remove the pastry from the oven again and add the remainder of the syrup. Return to the oven for 5 minutes.

Remove from the oven.

Blue Cheese Cake

with Grape Sauce
Inspired by Roy Guste, Jr.

Preheat oven to 375°
Makes 1 9" cake

CRUST:
1½ c graham cracker crumbs
½ c unbleached flour
⅓ c granulated sugar
1 t cinnamon
½ c butter
1 egg

FILLING:
20 oz. cream cheese
5 oz. blue cheese
1 c sour cream
⅓ c cream
⅔ c granulated sugar
4 eggs
1 T brandy or cognac
1 t vanilla extract

SAUCE:
2 lb. seedless green grapes
½ c honey
1 c granulated sugar
juice of 1 lemon
¼ c cognac or brandy
2 c water

To make the crust: Combine the graham cracker crumbs, flour, sugar, and cinnamon in a bowl. Blend into this mixture the butter, which has been softened. Add the egg and stir until a mouldable dough is formed. Press about ⅓ of this dough into a 9" springform pan to evenly cover the bottom. Bake in a preheated oven for 10 minutes. Remove from oven. When cool, press the remainder of the dough evenly around the sides of the pan. Lower the oven temperature to 250°.

To make the filling: Whip the cream cheese until soft. Crumble the blue cheese into the cream cheese. Whip until all the lumps of blue cheese are blended smoothly into the mixture. Add the sour cream, then the cream, then the sugar, beating until smooth after each addition. Add the eggs, one at a time, again beating until the mixture is evenly blended. The cognac and vanilla are added last. After stirring them in, pour the filling mixture into the springform. Bake in the 250° preheated oven for about 1½ hours. The cheesecake should be light golden, and set in the center, but not cracked or brown.
Allow to cool to room temperature before refrigerating. It is best to remove pan and serve after 24 hours. Make sure the cake has cooled thoroughly before adding the optional green grape sauce.

To make the sauce: Wash the grapes and remove all of the stems. Mash the grapes, or puree in a blender. Combine all the ingredients in a sauce pan and reduce over a low flame until it becomes the consistency of an thick sauce. Pour over the top of the cheese cake when cool.

Bread Pudding

with Rum Sauce

Preheat oven to 375°
Makes 8 servings

PUDDING:
5 c cubed, stale
  bread
2 t baking soda
½ c raisins
½ c granulated sugar
¼ c pineapple juice
¼ c rum
1 t vanilla extract
½ c milk or cream
½ t nutmeg

RUM SAUCE:
¾ c brown sugar
¼ c honey
⅜ c butter
2 T rum
1 T Grand Marnier
1 t vanilla extract

To make the pudding: Traditionally this pudding is made with white bread, but any kind will work. After the bread cubes have completely dried, sprinkle the baking soda over them and toss until the soda coats the cubes. Add the raisins to this dry mix and toss again.

In a mixing bowl, beat the eggs until light and creamy. Add the sugar, and then the milk, and beat until light. Add the vanilla and nutmeg. Stir in the bread cube mixture. While mixing this, slowly add the juice. Add the rum in the same manner. Allow the mixture to sit for a few minutes for the bread to absorb the liquid.

Oil 8 individual moulds or one large mould. Fill about ¾ full. Set in a pan of water. Place in the oven. Baking time should be about 25 minutes. For a large pan about 40 minutes is required. Allow to cool before removing from pans. Turn onto a serving platter or individual dessert plates.

To make the sauce: Heat the butter, brown sugar, and the honey in a saucepan over a medium flame. Stir while heating until they boil. Remove from burner. Stir in the rum, Grand Marnier, and the vanilla. Spoon over the puddings and serve while the sauce is hot.

Cannolis

(or as we spell them: knowles)
Enza Macri

Makes 18

FILLING:

3 c ricotta

1¼ c granulated sugar

2 t vanilla extract

optional: ¼ c grated
  semi-sweet
  chocolate

SHELLS:

3 c unbleached flour

¼ c granulated sugar

1 t cinnamon

¼ t salt

3 T butter

2 eggs

2 T white vinegar

2 T water

finely chopped
  pistachios

powdered sugar

This recipe is the only incidence of deep frying which you will find in this book. The irresistability of these pastries has called for a waiving of my standards. There is much preparation and effort needed for this recipe. Read the recipe carefully before starting. It is all worthwhile.

To make the filling: Combine the ricotta, sugar, and vanilla and whip until smooth. The grated chocolate may be folded into the filling mixture if desired. Refrigerate the filling until ready to use.

To make the shells: Combine in a bowl the flour, sugar, salt and cinnamon. With a fork or pastry blender, cut in the butter until it is in tiny pieces. Next, cut in the eggs. Measure the water and vinegar together and add it to the dough one spoonful at a time. Turn the dough onto a lightly floured board and knead for 5 minutes. Wrap the dough in waxed paper and refrigerate for at least ½ hour.

In a deep saucepan or deep fryer heat vegetable oil to 360°.

Make an oval pattern from cardboard or some substantial paper which is 6"x4½". Roll the chilled dough ⅛" thick on a floured surface. Using the pattern, cut the dough into as many ovals as possible. Before placing in the deep frying oil, these shells must be loosely wrapped, slightly overlapping, around dowel rods 6" long and 1" in diameter. An old broom handle, washed and cut in lengths, works just perfectly. Use an egg wash to make the overlap stick to itself. Fry the shells until golden, turning often. Remove from the oil and cool on paper towels or something absorbent.

Make sure the shells are completely cool before filling. After the shells are full, dip the ends in the pistachios. Dust the tops with powdered sugar.

Chocolate Eclairs

In memory of Jug Bacon

Preheat oven to 400°
Makes 18

CUSTARD:
⅔ c granulated sugar
6 T cornstarch
½ t salt
6 egg yolks
3 c milk
1½ t vanilla extract
2 T butter
1 c heavy cream

SHELLS:
1 c water
¼ c butter
⅛ t salt
1 c unbleached flour
5 eggs, at room
   temperature

GLAZE:
¼ c cocoa
½ c water
powdered sugar

To make the custard: Measure into the top half of a double boiler the sugar, cornstarch, and salt. Stir the egg yolks into this, one at a time. Gradually add the milk stirring constantly to avoid lumps. Add the vanilla. Place the bowl of custard mixture over the bottom part of its double boiler and, over heat, stir until the custard is thick. Remove from the heat and stir in the butter. Cool and then refrigerate. Just before filling the shells, whip the cream to ultimate stiffness and fold into the custard.

To make the shells: Bring to a boil in a saucepan the cup of water and the butter. Remove from heat and rapidly stir in the flour, all at one time. Add the eggs, one at a time, beating well after each addition. Spoon the batter into oval shapes about 5"x1"x½", on a lightly oiled tray. (It is easier, perhaps, to pipe the batter from a pastry bag, rather than spooning.) The shells hold a better shape when baked on parchment. Quickly put the tray into the oven. Bake until browned, which takes approximately 30 minutes. Remove from the oven, and allow the shells to cool before slitting the tops and removing the pulp. Fill with the chilled custard.

To make the glaze: Stir together the water and cocoa and add powdered sugar until you have a thick, but still liquid, consistency. Pour over the pastries.

Chocolate Soufflé

Preheat oven to 400°
Makes 4 servings

3 T butter
6 eggs
⅛ t salt
3 T unbleached flour
1¼ c milk
1½ ounces
  unsweetened
  chocolate
4 T light rum
2 t vanilla extract
6 T granulated sugar

butter
granulated sugar
whipping cream

Prepare an 8" souffle dish by adding a collar made of aluminium foil, which is pinned at the overlap and tied onto the dish with a string. Butter the dish and the collar and dust with granulated sugar.

Separate the eggs, putting the whites in a bowl large enough for whipping and the yolks in a cup. Scald the milk and remove from heat.

Melt the 3 T butter in a saucepan over a low heat. Gradually stir in the flour and cook for 2 minutes, stirring constantly, without browning the mixture. Gradually stir in the milk and stir over the burner until thickened. Add the chocolate squares and stir until melted. Remove from the heat and beat in the egg yolks, one at a time. Stir over the heat, once again until thickened. Remove from heat and stir in the sugar, salt, vanilla, and rum. Set the mixture aside.

Whip the egg whites until stiff. Stir about ¼ of them into the sauce. Fold the rest into the sauce carefully. Transfer the sauce to the souffle dish with a ladle, instead of pouring it.

Place the souffle dish in the 400° preheated oven, lower the temperature to 375°, and do not disturb for 30 minutes. Beat the whipping cream during the baking time. After removing from the oven, remove the collar and serve smothered in whipped cream.

Linzertorte

Bart Shumaker

Preheat oven to 300°
Makes 1 9" tart

⅔ c hazelnuts
1 c butter
¾ c granulated sugar
½ t vanilla extract
1½ c unbleached
  flour
1 T cinnamon
2 t baking powder
1 c raspberry
  preserves

powdered sugar

Roast the hazelnuts on a dry pan in the oven for 10 minutes. After they have cooled, roll them in a clean, dry towel to remove the skins. Pureé the nuts in a food processor.

Thoroughly cream the butter and sugar. Add the vanilla extract.

Mix the nuts, cinnamon, and baking powder into the flour. Add this dry mix gradually to the dough. Mix until evenly blended.

Refrigerate the dough for 1 hour. Press about ⅔ of the dough into the tart pan. Roll the remaining dough on a floured board and cut into strips about ¾" wide. Spread the preserves into the tart shell. Lattice the strips over the top.

Bake for about 35 minutes, or until the crust is nicely browned. After the tart has cooled, remove from the pan and dust with powdered sugar before serving.

Lemon Sponge Pudding

Mom

Preheat oven to 325°
Serves 4 delicately

3 eggs
¾ c granulated sugar
3 T unbleached flour
3 T lemon juice
2 T orange juice
3 T finely grated
   lemon peel
2 T finely grated
   orange peel
⅛ t salt

½ pint whipping
   cream
½ vanilla extract
2 T powdered sugar

Prepare and set aside the citrus juices and the grated peel. Separate the eggs. In a mixing bowl beat the yolks. Combine with the sugar and whip until light. Alternately add the flour and the juices until a smoothly blended mixture is achieved. Stir in the salt.

Beat the egg whites until stiff. Fold delicately into the lemon mixture. Ladle this carefully into a buttered glass baking dish. Set the glass dish in a pan of hot water. Place in the preheated oven and bake for approximately ½ hour. The pudding will be light golden on top.

Remove from oven and chill well before serving time.

Whip the cream until almost stiff, adding the vanilla and sugar just before finishing whipping.

Serve in bowls with plenty of whipped cream.

Too Chocolate Chocolate

Preheat oven to 375°
Makes 1 10" pie

CRUST:
2 c graham cracker crumbs
⅔ c unbleached flour
¼ c cocoa
½ c granulated sugar
½ c butter
1 egg

FILLING:
16 oz. cream cheese
⅔ c granulated sugar
3 eggs
⅔ c cream
1 T triple sec
2 T crème de cacao
1 t vanilla extract
¼ c cocoa

MOUSSE:
3 egg whites at room temperature
1½ c cream
1 T crème de cacao
1 t vanilla extract
3 T cocoa
⅓ c granulated sugar
½ pt. whipping cream
3 T powdered sugar
chocolate shavings

To make the crust: Combine the graham cracker crumbs, flour, cocoa, and sugar in a bowl. Into this blend the softened butter. Add the egg and beat until a dough is formed. Press this dough into a 10" pie pan. Perforate with a fork in several places. Bake for 10 minutes in the preheated oven. Remove from oven. Reduce oven temperature to 250°.

To make the filling: Whip the cream cheese until it is soft and smooth. Add the sugar and beat until smooth. Add the eggs, one at a time, until they are incorporated into the mixture, then whip for a few minutes. Sprinkle in the cocoa while beating very slowly. Beat until all lumps are gone. Gradually add the cream, and then the triple sec, creme de cacao, and vanilla. Pour into the crust and bake until set in a 250° oven. Baking time should be about an hour. Remove from oven and allow to cool to room temperature. Then refrigerate.

To make the mousse: Beat the egg whites until stiff, then set them aside. Whip the cream until it forms peaks. Slowly add the sugar, and then the cocoa. After this is smooth, add the creme de cacao and the vanilla. Fold the egg whites into the cream mixture.

After the filling has cooled, score the top a few times. This will allow the mousse layer to adhere more easily. Smooth the mousse evenly over the whole pie. Refrigerate.

Top this with a layer of whipped cream and some chocolate shavings before serving.

Cheesecake Brujaja

Preheat oven to 375°
Makes 1 9" cake

CRUST:

⅓ c granulated sugar

1½ c unbleached
flour

1½ t finely grated
lemon peel

¼ t cinnamon

¼ t ginger

⅝ c butter

2 egg yolks, slightly
beaten

1 t molasses

½ t vanilla extract

FILLING:

32 ounces cream
cheese

⅔ c sour cream

1⅓ c granulated sugar

4 eggs

2 egg yolks

2 T unbleached flour

½ t salt

¾ t finely grated
lemon peel

1 t vanilla extract

To make the crust: Combine in a bowl the sugar, flour, lemon peel, cinnamon, and ginger. Blend into this the softened butter. Then stir in the egg yolks, vanilla, and molasses. Press ½ of this crust mixture into the bottom of a springform pan. Bake in the preheated oven for 10 minutes. When cool, press the remaining ½ of the crust dough onto the sides of the springform pan.

To make the filling: Whip the cream cheese until soft. Add the sour cream and the sugar and mix until smooth. Add the eggs, one at a time, alternately with the flour, and then the yolks with the vanilla, salt, and lemon peel.

After the crust has been pressed into the pan, pour in the filling. Place in the oven, and after 10 minutes, lower the heat to 250°. Bake for 1 more hour. Remove from the oven, cool slowly, and refrigerate until completely cooled before removing the springform.

Scones

Preheat oven to 425°
Makes about 3 dozen

3½ c unbleached
  flour
1½ T baking powder
⅓ c granulated sugar
1 t salt
⅝ c butter
⅔ c cream
4 eggs

1 egg, beaten
½ c powdered sugar

Sift the dry ingredients (except powdered sugar) into a bowl. Cut the butter into this until well blended. Form a well in the center of the dough. In a small bowl beat together the eggs and cream. Pour this into the well and incorporate by tossing with 2 forks, as you would a salad, until lightly mixed.

Pat the dough gently onto a floured board, about ½" thick. Cut with cookie cutters, or cut into diamond shapes. Transfer to an oiled tray, brush with the beaten egg, and sprinkle with powdered sugar.

Place in the preheated oven, turn the temperature down to 375°, and bake 15 minutes or until golden.

SQUARES & BARS

Birdfood Bars

Preheat oven to 350°
Makes 2 dozen

1 cup honey
⅓ c peanut butter
1½ t vanilla extract
¼ t almond extract
½ c hot water
4½ c sesame seeds
⅔ c sliced almonds
2½ c shredded
  coconut
1 t salt
¾ c unbleached flour

Combine the honey, peanut butter, vanilla, almond extract, and hot water and beat until smooth and creamy. Add all of the dry ingredients and stir.

Press this mixture into an oiled and papered pan 9"x13". Use cold water on your hands to prevent dough from sticking.

Bake in a 350° oven for 25 minutes. The mix will be lightly browned. Cut into bars when almost cool.

Brownies

Preheat oven to 375°
Makes 2 dozen

1 c butter
7 eggs
3 c granulated sugar
1 c cocoa
2 t vanilla
¾ c walnuts
2¼ c unbleached
    flour

Cream together the butter, eggs, and sugar. This is the critical step. In an electric mixer this step takes at least 5 minutes.

Add the vanilla, walnuts, and cocoa and stir briefly at the slowest speed. It is important to remember that the air whipped into the eggs is the only ingredient that will make the brownies rise. Any extra beating after the first step is detrimental to the finished product.

Add the flour and stir only until it is evenly mixed. Pour the batter into a well oiled pan about 9" by 13". Spread evenly in the pan. Place in the oven and immediately turn the temperature to 325°. Baking time is about 35 minutes. The brownies are done when they bounce back after a soft touch in the center.

Brownies can be cut without tearing if you wait until they are cool.

Butterscotch Squares

Ronnie Bator's Mother

Preheat oven to 375°
Makes 2 dozen

1¼ c butter
5 eggs
5 c brown sugar
½ t salt
2 t vanilla extract
1¾ c roasted cashews
1 T baking powder
5⅔ c unbleached
  flour

Whip together until light the butter, eggs, and brown sugar. Add to this the salt, vanilla, and roasted cashews. Stir until blended. It is not essential to roast the nuts before adding to the mixture, but the enhancement of the flavor makes the effort worthwhile. Add the baking powder and flour and stir until thoroughly mixed. Spread this fairly dense mixture in a 10"x15" cake pan which has been oiled and floured.

Lower the oven temperature to 325° immediately after placing the squares in the oven. Baking time is about 30 minutes. Be careful not to overbake.

These are good with chocolate or butterscotch chips.

Cream Cheese Brownies

Shelly Shapiro

Preheat oven to 350°
Makes 1 dozen

4 ounces semi-sweet chocolate
5 T butter
3 ounces cream cheese
1 c granulated sugar
3 eggs
½ c plus 1 T unbleached flour
1½ t vanilla extract
½ t baking powder
½ t salt
¼ t almond extract
½ c chopped walnuts

In a small saucepan melt the chocolate with 3 T butter. Use low heat and stir continually to avoid scorching. Set this aside to cool.

To make the cheese layer, cream together 3 ounces of cream cheese and 2 T butter. Gradually add ¼ c of sugar and whip until fluffy. Blend in 1 egg and ½ t vanilla. Stir in 1 T flour and then set aside.

To finish the chocolate layer, beat together 2 eggs with ¾ c sugar. Blend into this the cooked chocolate mixture, 1 t vanilla, almond extract, and chopped walnuts. Next add salt, baking powder, and ½ c flour.

Spread ½ the chocolate mixture in a 9"x9" oiled pan. Over this, spread the cheese mixture. On top, add the last half of the chocolate. With a knife, marbleize the batter, then bake for 35 to 40 minutes. When the center bounces back after a slight tap, the brownies are done.

Chewy Peanut Fingers

Alicia Donaldson

Makes about 2 dozen

1 c crunchy peanut butter

¼ c honey

2 t vanilla extract

½ t salt

1½ c powdered milk

½ c powdered sugar

1 c finely chopped peanuts

In a bowl mix the peanut butter, honey, and vanilla. Add the salt, powdered milk, and powdered sugar. Stir well. Shape into fingers and roll in the finely chopped nuts. This quick energy snack can be stored in the refrigerator.

Date Bars

Mom

Preheat oven to 350°

Makes 2 dozen

3 eggs

¾ c granulated sugar

1½ c chopped dates

1 c chopped walnuts

1 t vanilla extract

¼ salt

1 t baking powder

1¼ c unbleached flour

powdered sugar

Thoroughly mix the eggs and the sugar. Add to this the dates, walnuts, vanilla, and salt. Next, add the flour and the baking powder at the same time. Mix well until even textured. Pour the batter into a 9"x13" baking pan, which has been oiled and lined with paper.

Bake for 30 minutes.

While still warm, cut into bars and roll in powdered sugar.

Healthy Fingers

Preheat oven to 325°
Makes 2 dozen

½ c honey
½ c peanut butter
1 T oriental sesame oil
1 t vanilla extract
½ c chopped pecans
1 T unbleached flour
2 T bran
¼ c raisins
1 c rolled oats
2 c toasted sesame
  seeds

Toast the sesame seeds on a dry pan in the oven until golden, stirring occasionally. This not only enhances the flavor, but also makes the sesame seeds more easily digestible.

Beat together the honey, peanut butter, sesame oil, and the vanilla. Add to this all of the dry ingredients except the sesame seeds, and blend.

Chill the mixture for an hour. Shape into slender fingers and roll in the toasted sesame seeds. Store in the refrigerator.

Lebkuchen

Preheat oven to 350°
Makes 2 dozen

1 c honey
1 c molasses
1½ c brown sugar
2 eggs
1 T grated lemon peel
2 T lemon juice
2 t cinnamon
1 t cloves
2 t nutmeg
1 c walnuts
1 t baking soda
5½ c unbleached
  flour

In a bowl, combine the honey, molasses, brown sugar, and eggs. Whip until the color lightens. Add the lemon peel, lemon juice, cinnamon, cloves, nutmeg, and walnuts. Stir. The last ingredients to be added are flour and baking soda. Mix thoroughly.

This fairly substantial dough should be patted evenly into a 9" by 13" baking pan which has been oiled and lined with paper. Bake for 35 minutes. Glaze with the Lebkuchen Glaze while still hot. Cut into squares after completely cooled.

SWEET BREADS

Apple Nut Bread

Ronnie Bator's Mother's Son

Preheat oven to 325°

Makes 3 medium loaves

1 c butter

2 c granulated sugar

3 eggs

1 T cinnamon

2 t vanilla extract

3 medium apples finely chopped

2 c walnuts

1½ t baking soda

½ t salt

3 c unbleached flour

Thoroughly cream the butter, sugar, and eggs. Add to this the cinnamon, vanilla, finely chopped apples, and the walnuts. Stir well. In a separate bowl, sift together the flour, baking soda, and salt. Blend these into the batter. This batter will be very stiff.

Divide this evenly among 3 loaf pans, well oiled and papered. Bake these in a preheated oven about 1¼ hours. Testing may be done with a toothpick.

After removing from the oven, allow a few moments before taking the loaves from the pans. Glaze while still hot. Cool on a wire rack.

This recipe is created in the 3-loaf size because it is so good, it disappears like magic.

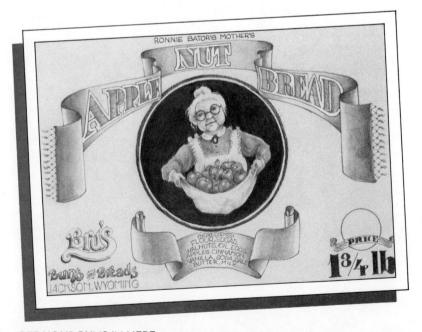

Apricot Bread

Preheat oven to 300°
Makes 2 loaves

1⅓ c dried apricots
1 c water
3 eggs
⅓ c oil
¾ c granulated sugar
1 t vanilla extract
2 c unbleached flour
1½ T baking powder
½ t salt
⅔ c pecan pieces

Place the apricots and the water in a small, covered pan. Cook on a low heat until soft.

Thoroughly cream the eggs, oil, and sugar. Add the vanilla and the cooked apricots. Beat until light.

Mix the dry ingredients, including the pecans. Gradually add these to the batter. Mix until smooth.

Pour the batter into loaf pans that have been lightly oiled and lined with paper. Bake for 1 hour.

Remove from the pans and cool on a wire rack.

Banana Nut Bread

Jon Kronenberg's Aunt Marg Yochum

Preheat oven to 325°
Makes 2 loaves

½ c oil
1 c granulated sugar
2 eggs
3 ripe bananas
1 t cinnamon
½ t ground cloves
1 t baking soda
½ t baking powder
2 c unbleached flour
½ c chopped walnuts

Cream together the oil, sugar, and eggs. When this combination is fluffy, add the bananas, cinnamon, and cloves. Blend until the bananas are mashed.

Sift together the flour, baking soda, and baking powder. Stir the nuts into the dry ingredients. Gradually stir this dry mix into the batter. After smoothly blended, pour the batter into 2 loaf pans which have been oiled and lined with paper.

Bake about 1¼ hours. Test with a toothpick.

Remove from the pans and place on a wire rack. Brush the tops of the loaves with a glaze while still hot.

Boston Brown Bread

Grandma Jones

Preheat oven to 350°
Makes 2 loaves

¼ c molasses
¼ c granulated sugar
1 T butter
1 egg
1½ c buttermilk
½ t salt
1 c whole wheat flour
1 c unbleached flour
1 t baking soda
1 t baking powder
½ c raisins

Beat together the molasses, sugar, butter, and the egg. These should grow smooth and light as you whip.

Sift together both kinds of flour, baking powder, baking soda, and salt. Add the dry ingredients and the buttermilk alternately to the batter, mixing thoroughly. Stir in the raisins.

Pour the batter into 2 medium sized loaf pans which have been oiled and lined with paper. Place in oven and lower the heat to 300°. Bake approximately 1 hour. Test the loaves with a toothpick.

Remove from the oven and after a few moments take the loaves from the pans. Cool on a wire rack.

Coconut Bread

For an event at the
Contemporary Arts Center, New Orleans

Preheat oven to 325°
Makes 2 loaves

3 eggs
½ c oil
1 c granulated sugar
1⅓ c shredded
  coconut
1 t vanilla extract
½ t lemon extract
2⅓ c unbleached
  flour
1⅓ T baking powder
½ t salt
1 t cinnamon
½ t nutmeg
1¼ c milk

Thoroughly cream the eggs, oil, and sugar.
Add the coconut and the vanilla and lemon
extracts. Beat until light.

Stir the baking powder, salt, cinnamon, and
nutmeg into the flour. Add this dry mix to the
batter, alternately with the milk.

Pour into loaf pans that have been lightly oiled
and papered. Bake for about 1 hour.

Remove from the pans and cool on a wire
rack.

Cranberry Bread

Preheat oven to 325°
Makes 2 loaves

¼ c butter
1 c granulated sugar
1 egg
¾ c orange juice
1 T orange rind
2 c chopped
   cranberries
1½ t baking powder
½ t baking soda
2 c unbleached flour
1 c chopped walnuts

Begin by chopping and measuring the cranberries. Set aside. Next, prepare and measure the orange juice. Add the grated orange rind to the juice, then set aside until needed.

Thoroughly cream the butter, sugar, and egg. When this mixture is light, add the cranberries and stir.

Sift together the flour, baking powder, baking soda, and salt. Stir the walnuts into the dry ingredients. Add the dry mix to the batter alternately with the orange juice and stir well. This batter will be quite stiff.

Divide the batter equally between 2 loaf pans which have been oiled and papered. Bake until a testing toothpick can be removed clean from the center of the loaves. Baking time is about 1 hour and 15 minutes. Remove from the pans and cool on a wire rack. Glaze while still warm.

Date Nut Bread

Dean Betts' Aunt Alberta

Preheat oven to 350°
3 medium loaves

¼ c butter
1¼ c granulated sugar
2 eggs
2 t vanilla extract
2 c chopped dates
2 oranges
2 t baking soda
2 t baking powder
¾ t salt
4¾ c unbleached
  flour
2 c walnuts

Prepare the oranges by rolling them on a counter under the pressure of your hand. Cut them in half and extract the juice. Pour this juice into a 2 cup measure. Grate the peels and add this to the juice. Add enough water to the cup to total 2 cups.

In a mixing bowl, thoroughly cream the butter, sugar, and eggs. When this mixture is light, stir in the vanilla and the dates and blend well.

Sift together the flour, baking powder, baking soda, and the salt. Stir into this dry mix the chopped walnuts. Alternately add the dry ingredients and the orange juice until all the ingredients are combined and well blended.

Pour the batter into 3 medium loaf pans which have been oiled and papered. After placing in the oven, reduce the temperature to 300°. Bake about 1½ hours. Test the loaves with a toothpick. Wait a few moments before removing from pans. Glaze while still hot. Cool on a wire rack. The orange and date combination of flavors is tops.

Irish Soda Bread

Jackie NcNulty Haber

Preheat oven to 375°
Makes 1 large loaf

4 c unbleached flour
¼ c granulated sugar
1 t salt
1 t baking powder
1 t baking soda
2 T caraway seeds
¼ c butter
2 c raisins
1 egg
1⅓ c buttermilk
1 egg yolk

Sift together the flour, sugar, salt, baking powder, and baking soda into a bowl. Stir in the caraway seeds. Cut in the butter until the mixture looks like coarsely-ground grain. Stir in raisins. Beat the egg into the buttermilk, then stir into the dry ingredients, barely combining them.

Turn the dough onto a lightly-floured board and knead lightly until the dough is smooth. Shape into a ball and place in a well-oiled 2 quart round casserole. With a serrated blade, slash the top of the loaf with an X. Brush the loaf with the egg yolk which has been beaten with 1 T water.

Bake for about 1 hour or until a toothpick comes out clean from the center. Allow the loaf to set for 10 minutes before removing from the pan. Cool on a wire rack. Cut into quarters, then slice to serve.

Lemon Pecan Bread

Preheat oven to 325°
Makes 1 loaf

⅓ c butter
1 c granulated sugar
2 eggs
¼ t almond extract
1 T grated lemon peel
3 T lemon juice
½ c milk
1 t baking powder
½ t salt
1½ c unbleached
   flour
½ c chopped
   pecans

Thoroughly cream the butter, sugar, and eggs. Add to this the almond extract, lemon juice, and grated rind.

Sift together the flour, baking powder, and salt. Stir into this dry mixture the pecans. Add the dry mix to the batter alternately with the milk until all are evenly blended. This batter is quite fluid and perishable. It is important to minimize the time between adding the milk and getting the loaf into the oven.

Pour the batter into an oiled and papered pan and bake about 1 hour or until done. Test with a toothpick.

Remove from the pans and cool on a wire rack. Glaze while still warm.

Pumpkin Bread

Preheat oven to 325°
Makes 1 loaf

⅓ c butter
1 c granulated sugar
2 eggs
1 c pumpkin, fresh or
  canned
⅓ c water
½ t vanilla extract
½ t cinnamon
½ t nutmeg
2 c unbleached flour
1 t baking soda
¼ t baking powder
¾ t salt
½ c chopped pecans
½ c raisins

Cream the butter, sugar and eggs thoroughly. Stir in the pumpkin, water, vanilla, cinnamon, and nutmeg. Beat until smooth.

Sift together the flour, baking powder, and salt. Add to this dry mix the nuts and the raisins. Gradually incorporate this dry mixture into the batter.

Pour the batter into 2 oiled and papered loaf pans and bake for about 1 hour. Allow a few moments to cool before removing from pans. Cool on a wire rack. Glaze while hot.

Zucchini Bread

Mrs. Worrall Hess, Sr.

Preheat oven to 325°
Makes 2 loaves

1¾ c granulated sugar
4 eggs
1 c vegetable oil
1 t vanilla extract
2 c grated zucchini
3½ c unbleached
  flour
1 t baking powder
1½ t baking soda
1½ t salt
1 T cinnamon
1 c raisins
1 c walnuts, chopped

Beat the eggs. Add the sugar and oil, then cream until smooth and light. With a few strokes, blend into this mixture the vanilla and the grated zucchini.

In a separate mixing bowl, measure the flour, baking soda, baking powder, salt, and cinnamon. Stir these together. Pour the walnuts and the raisins into this dry mix. Stir once again.

Gradually add the dry ingredients to the batter, mixing until an even texture is obtained. Pour the batter into 2 loaf pans, which have been lightly oiled and papered. Bake about an hour, or until the loaves are evenly browned, and bounce back when tapped in the center.

After removing the finished loaves from the pans, cool on a wire rack.

BREADS & ROLLS

The Wheats

**(Unannounced guests with dinner ringing
and the phone burning)**

Undoubtedly upon your mind
   the tragic wheats, their presence find.
Don't think concern is yours alone,
   I sleep frustrated now at home.
At first I held my hopes so high—
The bubbling softly whispered sigh
Gave every reasonable indication
Tonight the breads would rise to occasion.
Things looked so good for a while,
To the breads I betrayed a satisfied smile;
And sitting back in a moment's applause,
The loaves .abandoned the bakery's cause.
Maliciously, they had the gall,
When placed in the oven to mockingly fall.
Heartfelt dismay was mine half an hour later.
My wheats held all the beauty of an old alligator.

Much as I wish to clutch at fate
I fear I put them in too late;
so much preliminary size
undoubtedly was all they'd rise.
What can I say for all my yearning,
Bru, but, the wheats I am still learning.

S. Doug Hettinger

Beer Bread

Denny Ash

Bake at 350°
Makes 2 loaves

1½ c warm beer
⅓ c bacon grease
⅓ c molasses
1 T caraway seeds
2 T yeast
⅓ c water
6 c whole wheat flour
2 t salt

Combine in a large mixing bowl the beer, bacon grease, molasses, and caraway seeds. Make sure they are warm enough to promote the growth of the yeast colony.

Dissolve the yeast in the water. When the volume has doubled, pour it into the mixing bowl. Immediately add 3 cups of the wheat flour and beat for at least 100 strokes. Cover and set this batter aside for 15 minutes.

Beat the mixture down to its original size. Add the salt and gradually blend in the remainder of the flour. When the dough becomes too stiff to stir, turn onto a lightly-floured surface and knead for 10 minutes. Return the dough to the bowl. Oil the surface, cover, and allow to rise until doubled.

Punch down the dough. Knead until smooth and shape into loaves. Place the loaves in oiled, lightly-floured pans. When the loaves have doubled, bake for about 40 minutes. After they are done, remove from the pans and cool on a wire rack.

Cardamom Rolls

(Inspiration at the Sea of Cortez)

Bake at 350°
Makes 2 dozen

2 c water
⅔ c oil
½ c honey
2 eggs
3 T yeast
1 T cardamom
1 T cinnamon
1 t salt
5 c unbleached flour
4 c rye flour

In a large mixing bowl, combine the water, honey, and oil. Slowly stir in the yeast, making sure it is dissolved. When the yeast rises to the surface, add the cardamom, cinnamon, the beaten eggs, and ½ of each kind of flour. Beat the batter for 100 strokes, then let rest for ten minutes.

Beat the batter down to its original size. Add the salt, and gradually work in the remaining flour. When a kneadable consistency is reached, turn the dough onto a lightly-floured surface and knead for 5 minutes. Return the dough to the bowl and lightly oil the crust before covering and allowing to rise for 30 minutes.

Punch down the dough. Gently knead to remove airholes. Shape into little round rolls. Place the rolls on an oiled tray. When the rolls have at least doubled size, bake in a preheated oven for about 25 minutes. Remove the rolls from the tray while hot, and cool on a wire rack.

The flavors in these rolls blend extremely well with a variety of sea foods.

Cheese Bread

Bruce Littlefield

Preheat oven to 375°
Bake at 350°
Makes 1 loaf

2 T butter
1 T honey
4 T unbleached flour
1 c milk
1¼ c grated cheddar
1 T yeast
¼ c water
3 c unbleached flour
1 t salt

In a saucepan or double boiler melt the butter. Stir in the honey. Gradually add the 4 T flour, stirring to ensure there are no lumps in the mixture. Continue stirring and add the milk slowly. Cook this sauce until thickened, stirring constantly. Add the grated cheese and continue stirring until the cheese is melted, and a thick, smooth sauce is achieved. Allow the sauce to cool until warm to the touch.

Soften the yeast in the ¼ c of water. After it has started to foam, pour the yeast mixutre into a large mixing bowl. Stir into it a little flour. Next, add the cheese sauce, and stir until smooth. Gradually add flour until the dough reaches a kneadable consistency, remembering to add the salt with the last flour. Turn this soft dough onto a floured surface and knead for 5 minutes. Return to the mixing bowl, cover and allow to rise until doubled.

Punch down the dough, knead until smooth, and shape into a loaf. Place the loaf in a slightly oiled pan, cover, and allow to rise until doubled.

Place the loaf in oven. After 5 minutes lower the oven temperture to 350°. Baking time is about 40 minutes more. Remove from the pan before cooling on a wire rack.

Dark Rye

Bake at 350°
Makes 2 loaves

2½ c water
3 T oil
2 T honey
¼ c molasses
2½ T yeast
3 T caraway seeds
¼ c cocoa
5 c unbleached flour
1 T salt
4 c rye flour

cornmeal

When using rye flour it is important to remember that it will not rise by itself. Rye flour does not have enough gluten to hold a bread structure together. For this reason it is mixed with another kind of flour. Rye should not be over-beaten, over-risen, or kneaded too long.

In a large mixing bowl, combine the water, honey, molasses, and oil. Stir briefly, and continue to do so while slowly adding the yeast. Stir until yeast is completely dissolved. While the yeast is growing undisturbed, and before it rises to the surface, measure the cocoa, caraway and ½ of each kind of flour. When the yeast does rise to the surface and begins to foam, add these ingredients. Beat until all are thoroughly mixed. Allow to rest 10 minutes before beating down to its original size. Stir in the salt. Gradually work in the rest of the flour. If more flour is needed, use unbleached, rather than rye. When a kneadable consistency is reached, knead long enough to create a smooth dough. This should take 3 to 5 minutes. Shape the dough evenly divided into round loaves. Set the loaves on a tray covered with cornmeal. "X" the tops with a serrated knife. Allow to rise until doubled before baking for about 40 minutes. Whap the loaves and listen for a hollow tone to ensure they are done. Cool on a wire rack.

English Muffins

Cook in an oiled skillet
Makes 1 dozen

1½ c scalded milk
1 T honey
1 T yeast
1 t salt
1 c whole wheat flour
2¼ c unbleached
  flour

cornmeal

Scald the milk, then pour it into a large mixing bowl. Stir in the honey. When the liquid has cooled to about 100°, stir in the yeast. Add the wheat flour and 1 c unbleached flour when the yeast rises to the surface. Beat 100 strokes. Let rest covered for 10 minutes. Add the salt and gradually work in the remaining flour. Knead lightly for 5 minutes. Return to the bowl, cover, and let rise for 20 minutes.

Punch down the dough. Place it on a counter covered with cornmeal. Dust the top with cornmeal. Roll the dough to ¾" thick. Cut into rounds approximately 4" in diameter. Cover these and let them rise for 15 minutes, or until doubled.

Using a metal spatula, carefully transfer to a medium hot, oiled skillet or grill. Turn often, remembering to handle gently, until they are browned on both sides. This will take about 15 minutes. Cool on a wire rack.

Egg Bagels

Bake at 375°
Makes 2 dozen

2½ c water
¼ c honey
2 T yeast
1 egg
2 t salt
12 c unbleached flour

OPTIONAL:
1 diced onion
poppy seeds
sesame seeds

Pour into a very large mixing bowl 2½ c of warm water. Dissolve the honey in this. Slowly pour in the yeast, while stirring. Let the yeast sit undisturbed while 6 c flour are measured. As soon as the yeast begins to rise to the surface, pour in the flour and stir until the mixture is smooth and shiny.

Allow to rise 10 minutes. Add the egg and salt and beat well. Gradually add the remaining flour, stirring until it becomes too difficult. When that happens, turn the dough onto a floured board and knead for 5 minutes. Cover the dough and allow it to rest a few minutes.

Choosing a pan with a large diameter. Fill with water, and bring to a boil. Add to this 1 T of salt.

To shape the bagels, divide the dough into equal pieces, and roll them in 3" balls. Poke a hole in the center of each, twirl around your fingers, and flatten by placing on a counter and pounding with the palm of your hand.

With tongs or a slotted spoon, place the bagels in the boiling water. After they rise to the surface they should remain in the water less than ½ a minute. Remove them from the water, and place them on an oiled tray. If you want seeds on the bagels, sprinkle them on before they dry. Bake 20 minutes until golden.

If onion bagels are desired, add one finely diced onion at the same time the salt and egg are added. This addition will necessitate adding more flour.

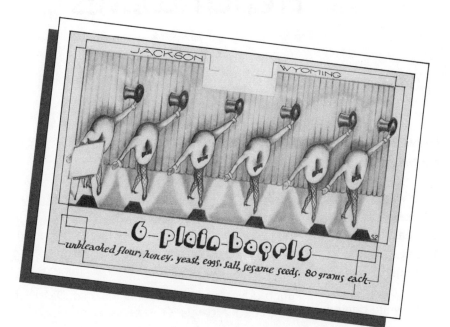

French Loaves

Makes 2 loaves
Bake at 400°

2½ c water
2 T honey
2 T yeast
1 t salt
7 c flour

1 egg white beaten
sesame seeds

In a large bowl dissolve the honey in the water. Stir in the yeast. When the yeast rises, add ½ the flour. Beat 50 strokes. Let rest 5 minutes.

Add the salt and stir down to its original size. Work in the remaining flour. Knead this fairly stiff dough for 10 to 15 minutes. Return to the bowl and oil the crust. Cover and let rise for 15 minutes. Punch the dough and let rise for 40 minutes.

Punch down and knead for 5 minutes. Divide the dough into 2 loaves. Cover and let rest for 10 minutes.

Shape into loaves. Place the loaves on an oiled tray. With a serrated knife slash the loaves diagonally every 2½", ¼" deep. Beat the egg white until foamy. Add to it 1 T water. Brush this over the loaves. Sprinkle with sesame seeds.

Let rise until doubled, which should take at least 1 hour. Place the loaves in a preheated oven. Place a few ice cubes in the oven. This moisture will help create a good crust. Baking time is about ½ hour. Remove from the oven when properly browned.

Logan Bread

Preheat oven to 275°
Makes 2 loaves

6 eggs
2 T oil
½ c honey
¼ c molasses
½ c maple syrup
2 c rye flour
2½ wheat flour
¼ c brown sugar
½ c powdered milk
½ c chopped pecans
⅔ c raisins
½ c coconut

Logan bread is an extremely substantial little item. It is the perfect bread to take on long and arduous expeditions. Not only is it compact and durable, its nutritional value is very high. It keeps for long periods of time.

In a large bowl, mix together all of the dry ingredients.

In a mixing bowl, beat the eggs so that they become frothy and light. Add the other liquids, one at a time, continuing to beat to form a well-blended mixture.

Gradually work in all of the dry ingredients to form a thick, sticky mixture. Transfer the dough to well-oiled loaf pans which have been lined with paper. Bake for about 2 hours. If the loaves appear to be browning too rapidly, reduce the heat to 225°. Test with a toothpick in the center. Cool on a wire rack, after removing the papers. Wrap well for freezing or travelling.

Light Rye

From a Wild Winds Inspiration

Bake at 350°
Makes 2 loaves

2 c water
¼ c oil
⅜ c honey
2½ T yeast
2 T dill weed
2 T dill seed
4 c unbleached flour
1 T salt
4 c rye flour

Combine in a large mixing bowl the water (which should be quite warm), oil, and honey. After the honey has been stirred to the point of dissolving, stir in the yeast. Before the yeast rises to the surface measure the dill weed, dill seed, and 2 c of each kind of flour. As the yeast surfaces pour in all of these ingredients and beat until smooth. Cover and set aside for 10 minutes.

Beat the batter down to its original size, then stir in the salt. Gradually add the remaining flour to form a soft, kneadable dough. Knead this dough on a floured surface until smooth and elastic. Return to the mixing bowl, oil the crust slightly, and cover. Let this rise until doubled, in a warm place. Punch the dough, knead slightly, and shape into loaves. Place the loaves in oiled, lightly floured pans. Cover and allow to rise. When the loaves have doubled, bake about 40 minutes. The loaves should sound hollow when tapped, and appear quite brown. Remove them from the oven. Remove from the pans. Cool on a wire rack.

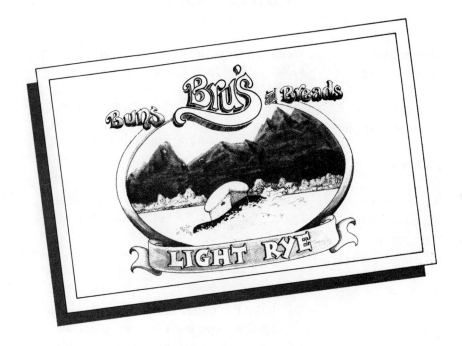

Buns Bru's and Breads

LIGHT RYE

Oatmeal Sunflower Millet Bread

Bake at 350°
Makes 2 loaves

2¼ c water
⅝ c safflower oil
½ c honey
2½ T yeast
1½ T salt
½ c rolled oats
¼ c hulled millet
¼ c sunflower seeds
6½ c whole wheat
  flour

Prepare a large mixing bowl by filling it with hot water whle you assemble the necessary ingredients. Empty the water and measure into the bowl the oil, honey, and water. Stir until the honey is dissolved. Sprinkle the yeast into the mixture while stirring. Continue stirring until the yeast is softened. Allow to sit undisturbed while measuring ½ of the flour.

After the yeast has risen to the surface and become foamy, pour in the flour and beat for at least 100 strokes. The batter will develop an elasticity and glossiness. Cover with a cloth and allow to rest in a warm place until doubled, about 20 minutes.

Stir down the batter until it is approximately its original size. Add the salt, oats, sunflower seeds, and the millet. Blend these into the batter. Measure another 3 cups of flour. Add about 1 cup of flour to the batter. Stir in. Keep adding flour while stirring until the batter becomes a dough too stiff to stir. Turn onto a board and knead for 10 minutes. The amount of flour used will vary, due to atmospheric conditions. The dough should remain moist, but not sticky; firm, but not dry. During the kneading process the dough will absorb more flour. Return this dough to the bowl. Lightly oil the crust, cover, and allow to rise undisturbed until at least doubled.

Punch the dough down, and knead it for about 5 minutes. Cut the dough in half and shape it into loaves. Place these loaves in oiled, lightly floured pans. Let rise until slightly more than doubled. Bake until a hollow sound is made by tapping the loaves, or approximately 40 minutes.

Remove from the pans and cool on a rack.

Whole Wheat Bread

My recipe for whole wheat bread is actually the beginning of the evolution which brought us all O.S.M. (oatmeal sunflower millet). The ingredients and procedures are identical, with one exception. More wheat flour is added instead of the grains at the point of last additions to the mixture. The dough will be smoother, of course, but it will have the same softness. Baking and all else remain the same.

Onion Rolls

Bake at 375°
Makes 1½ dozen

2 c water
⅓ c oil
3 T honey
1½ T yeast
8 c unbleached flour
⅔ c onions, finely
   diced
1 T salt

1 beaten egg

In a large mixing bowl, combine the water, oil and honey. After the honey is dissolved, stir in the yeast. When the yeast rises to the surface, stir in ½ the flour and beat for 50 strokes. Set aside, covered, for 10 minutes.

Add the finely diced onion and the salt and stir down to its original size. Gradually add the remaining flour to form a very soft dough. Turn this dough onto a floured surface and knead until smooth. The onions continually create more moisture. Flour must be added often to prevent the dough from becoming too sticky. Return the dough to the bowl, cover, and allow to rise until doubled.

Prepare an egg wash by beating an egg together with 2 T water. Punch down the dough. Knead long enough to rid the dough of air pockets, adding as much flour as necessary. Handle the dough very lightly. Shape the dough into ovals 5"x2½" which are smooth on top. Be sure the rolls are not more than ¾" thick. Place the rolls on an oiled baking sheet. Brush with the egg wash. Preheat the oven while the rolls double. Baking time will be approximately 25 minutes. When the rolls have started to brown, remove them from the oven and egg wash them again. Remove them to the oven until they become golden.

Remove from the trays and cool on a wire rack.

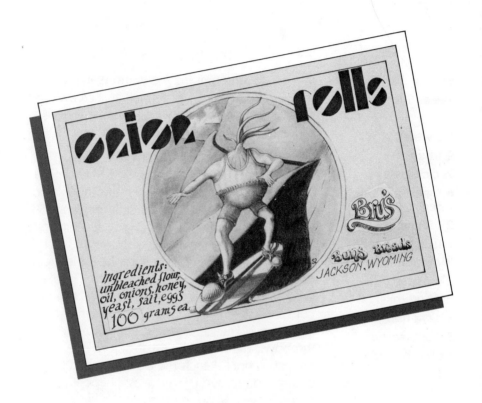

Ragbrod

Bake at 375°
Makes 2 loaves

1 c water
2 T butter
½ c molasses
6 T grated orange peel
2 T fennel seeds
2 T caraway seeds
¼ c water
2½ T yeast
2 c buttermilk
4 c rye flour
5 c unbleached flour
1 t baking soda
1 T salt

In a saucepan combine 1 c warm water, butter, molasses, oarange peel, fennel, and caraway seeds and bring to a boil. Allow time for this sauce to cool to 110° before continuing.

In a large mixing bowl dissolve the yeast in ¼ cup of warm water. After the yeast becomes foamy, add the buttermilk, then the sauce, and then ½ of each kind of flour. Beat for about 50 strokes. Allow this mixture to grow undisturbed for 10 minutes. After the rest, stir down the mixture. Sprinkle in the baking soda, salt and 1 cup of unbleached flour. Stir until smooth. Gradually work in the rest of the flours. When a kneadable consistency is reached, turn onto a lightly floured surface and knead for about 5 minutes. Return to the bowl. Lightly oil the crust before allowing to rise for ½ hour. Punch the dough. Knead long enough to remove the airholes. Shape into 2 round loaves. Slash the tops of the loaves with X's. Allow to rise until doubled. Bake about 40 minutes. The loaves may be sprayed or brushed with water while baking. Remove from the tray, and cool on a wire rack.

Spinach Loaf

Barbara Sanford Smith

Bake at 425° for 10
minutes then 350°

Makes 1 loaf

1½ c water
2 T olive oil
1½ T honey
1 T yeast
1 egg, beaten
1 finely minced
clove of garlic
4½ c flour
1 t salt

olive oil
grated romano
grated mozzarella
chopped spinach
diced onion
chopped olives

In a large bowl combine the water, olive oil, and honey. After the honey is dissolved, stir in the yeast. When the yeast rises to the surface, add the egg, salt and garlic. Gradually work in enough flour to make a soft dough.

Turn the dough onto a lightly floured counter and knead 5 minutes. Return to the bowl, oil the crust, cover, and let rise 15 minutes. Punch down.

On a floured counter, roll the dough into a rectangle ½" thick. Brush lightly with olive oil. The fillings are all optional. Cover the dough with grated cheese. Sprinkle with chopped fresh spinach, onions, and olives. Roll tightly, tucking all the edges under the roll. Place on a lightly oiled tray.

Preheat the oven to 425°. After 20 minutes place the loaf in the oven. After 10 minutes, reduce the heat to 350° and bake for another ½ hour or until browned. This may be eaten hot or cold.

Tortillas

Rhonda Robles Donaldson

**Makes 1 dozen
10" tortillas**

4 c flour
1 T salt
⅔ c bacon grease
1 c warm water

In a large mixing bowl measure the flour and salt. Mix together with your hands. Add the bacon grease and blend it into the flour by rubbing between your hands and fingers. The bacon grease should be quite well blended before adding the water. Form a well in the center of the flour. Pour the water into this well. Mix until a dough is formed. Depending on the weather, a little more water may be needed to attain a soft dough.

Turn onto a barely floured surface and knead for 10 minutes. Let the dough rest for 15 minutes, wrapped in a towel. Knead for a few moments more before it is ready to roll. Twist off about $\frac{1}{12}$ of the dough. Shape it with your fingers so that it is as flat and round as possible. Using a rolling pin, roll once over the tortilla and once back. Flip the tortilla over and rotate it ⅓ of a circle. Roll once, flip, and rotate again. Adequate flour should be used to prevent the tortilla from sticking to the rolling surface. Excess flour will easily brush off. By repeating the rolling, rotating process the tortilla will become very thin.

Heat a large cast iron skillet on a medium high fire. Cook the tortillas in this pan, dry and preheated, until light brown spots appear on both sides. Turn with tongs or a spatula. A translucent quality will appear while cooking. Good tortillas resemble craters on the moon to a vivid imagination. If the tortillas are well wrapped when cool, they will remain soft and delectable for days. They may be reheated in the same manner in which they were cooked.

SOURDOUGH

Sourdough Starter

2 c water
2 T sugar
2 T dry yeast
2 c unbleached flour

Heat the water to boiling, then allow to cool to about 100°. Stir in the sugar until dissolved. Gradually add the yeast, stirring until dissolved. Add the flour. Stir. Cover loosely.

I recommend a crock as a container for sourdough starter. It holds a more constant temperature than most containers. The crock should be more than twice as large as the volume of the starter.

The sugar is not necessary for the starter. It gives the starting yeast cells an immediately available food supply. It makes the process happen faster. If you are opposed to the use of sugar, leave it out. It will take longer.

After the starter has been made, feed it equal volumes of flour and water. Its consistency should be like that of a thick milkshake.

If you use your starter often, keep it at room temperature. Feed and water it a little every day. If you want it to grow faster or be more sour, keep it warmer. Above 140° will kill it.

If you want the starter to slow down or to keep longer between uses, refrigerate it. Make sure it returns to room temperature, and that you feed it before you use it.

Freezing will make it keep indefinitely. Freeze the starter in an airtight container much larger than the volume of the starter.

If it changes color or odor, throw it out. Wash the crock, and start again.

I think it's a great idea to freeze a portion of starter in case something happens to the part in use.

Changing the quality of water or the kind of flour will affect the starter. Those little one-celled animals like consistency.

There are many uses for sourdough. I have barely begun to experiment. It adds wonderful taste and texture to cakes, pancakes, waffles, and many breads. Discover some of your own.

Sourdough
French Bread

Bake at 500°
Makes 2 loaves

1 c water
1 T honey
1 T yeast
1 c sourdough starter
1 T salt
7½ to 8 c unbleached
  flour

cornmeal
1 beaten egg

In a large mixing bowl, dissolve the honey in the water, which should be quite warm. While stirring, slowly add the yeast. As the yeast beings to foam, pour in the sourdough starter. Immediately stir in the first half of the flour. When the texture is smooth, set aside to rise in a warm place. Cover to keep from drafts.

When the mixture has doubled, add the salt. Beat down. Gradually add flour. When stirring is no longer possible, turn onto a floured board and knead. Continue adding flour and kneading until dough is very stiff. Knead until smooth. Cover and set aside to rise until doubled. This dough will rise very slowly.

When the doubled size is achieved, punch down and knead again. If the dough has softened, add more flour. Shape into loaves. Place on trays sprinkled with cornmeal. Slash the tops with a series of parallel diagonals. Brush lightly with an egg wash made by beating an egg, then adding about 2 T of water, and beating again. Set aside to double once again.

Place in a preheated oven. Throw in some ice cubes, and shut the door. Baking time is approximately 25 minutes. Feel free to throw in more ice cubes. It helps make the loaves crustier.

Remove from the oven when brown. The loaves should sound hollow when tapped.

Sourdough Rye Bread

Bake at 475°
Makes 2 loaves

1½ c water
1½ T yeast
1 c sourdough starter
5–6 c rye flour
7–8 c unbleached
  flour
1½ T salt
2 T caraway seeds

cornmeal
1 beaten egg

Pour the warm water into a large mixing bowl. Stir while slowly adding the yeast. Continue stirring until dissolved. After a few minutes, when the yeast rises to the surface, add the sourdough starter. Next, add half of each kind of flour. Beat until smooth. Cover and set aside to double.

After the dough has doubled, add the caraway seeds and beat down. Add the salt with the next cups of flour. Stir in. Keep adding flour until it is impossible to stir. Turn onto a floured board, and continue adding flour until the dough is extremely stiff. Set aside, covered, to rise until doubled. This could take hours.

After the dough has risen, beat down. Knead. Shape into loaves. Set the loaves on trays covered with cornmeal. Slash the tops with a series of diagonal lines. Set aside to double.

Place the loaves in a preheated oven. Throw in a handful of ice cubes. Close the oven door. After about 20 minutes, remove the loaves from the oven. Brush lightly with an egg wash made by beating an egg, then adding about 2 T of water, and beating again. Return the loaves to the oven. Throw in another handful of ice cubes.

Bake until well browned and hollow sounding, which should take about 20 more minutes. Remove from oven and cool on a wire rack.

CANDY

Divinity

Jon Kronenberg

Makes 40 1" squares

⅓ c light corn syrup
¼ c water
1⅛ c granulated sugar
1 egg white
⅛ t salt
¼ c chopped pecans
½ t vanilla extract

powdered sugar

Bring the water and the corn syrup to a boil in a covered saucepan. Remove from the heat and stir in the sugar. Return to the heat and bring to a boil. Remove the cover and continue boiling without stirring, at as low a heat as possible while the boiling action continues. Remove from the heat when a drop of this syrup does not change shape even slightly when dropped into a glass of ice water.

Beat the egg white until stiff. Stir the egg white and the salt into the syrup mixture. Place the saucepan in a sink of cold water and continue stirring until the glossiness is gone.

Stir in the pecans and the vanilla. Pour the mixture onto a buttered stoneware platter. After it has cooled, the divinity may be cut, rolled in powdered sugar, and wrapped.

English Toffee

Becky Stone

**Makes 2 dozen
1" squares**

2 c unsalted butter
½ c water
2 c granulated sugar
1 T corn syrup
¾ c chopped almonds
1 oz. bitter chocolate
2 T granulated sugar

Bring to a boil in a covered saucepan the butter, water, and corn sryup. After this has boiled, remove from the heat and stir in the sugar until it has dissolved. Return to the heat, and again cover and bring to a boil. Remove cover and pour in the almonds. Reduce the heat to medium and continue boiling until the mixture smokes. It is important that the cover is removed to allow evaporation. It is also important not to stir.

Pour the smoking toffee onto a buttered stoneware platter, or a slab of marble, if you happen to have one.

Melt the chocolate square with 2 T sugar. Spread the chocolate over the toffee. Sprinkle with almonds which have been finely chopped. Cut when cooled.

Sesame Crunch

Preheat oven to 350°
Makes 1 dozen
1" squares

1½ sesame seeds
1½ c honey
1 T vinegar
¼ t salt

Place the sesame seeds on an oiled pan and bake for 15 minutes. Boil the honey, vinegar, and salt together until a drop of this syrup holds its shape when dropped into a glass of ice water. Pour the syrup over the sesame seeds, stir, and flatten. Cut into 1" squares while still warm.

Penuche

Makes 40 1" squares

¾ c light cream
2 T butter
1 c brown sugar
1½ c granulated sugar
1 t vanilla extract
½ c finely chopped walnuts

In a covered saucepan heat the butter and cream to boiling. Remove from the heat and stir in the sugars. Return to the heat and bring to a boil, again covered. When the sugar crystals on the sides of the pan dissolve, remove the cover, reduce the heat, and cook gently until a drop of the syrup holds its shape when dropped in a glass of ice water.

Cool without stirring until the pan feels lukewarm. Add the vanilla and walnuts. Beat with a wooden spoon until the mixture loses its gloss. Pour onto a buttered stoneware platter. Cut when cool.

CAKES & MUFFINS

Banana Cake

Preheat oven to 350°
Makes 2 9" layers

¾ c butter
1 c sugar
2 eggs
1 c bananas, mashed
1 t vanilla
1⅞ c unbleached
  flour
1 t salt
1 t baking soda
½ t cinnamon
¼ t cloves, ground
⅓ c milk

Thoroughly cream the butter and sugar. Add the eggs, one at a time, and beat until light. Add the cup of mashed bananas and the vanilla. Beat until smooth. Measure the flour by sifting it straight into the measuring cup and then stir in the salt, baking soda, cinnamon, and cloves.

Add this dry mix to the batter with the milk. Blend until evenly mixed.

Pour the batter into the cake pans, that have been lightly oiled, floured, and lined with paper. Bake for about 35 to 40 minutes or until the centers of the cakes bounce back after a light touch.

Basic Yellow Cake

Preheat oven to 350°
Makes 2 9" layers

¾ c butter
1½ c granulated sugar
3 eggs
1 t vanilla extract
1¼ c milk
½ t salt
2 t baking powder
3 c unbleached flour

Thoroughly cream the butter, sugar, and eggs. Blend in the vanilla.

Sift the flour before measuring. Stir the salt and baking powder into the flour. Add the milk and the dry ingredients alternately. Beat well. Pour evenly into two 9" layer pans which have been oiled and lined with paper.

Bake about 35 minutes or until the centers of the layers bounce back after a soft touch.

This basic cake may be frosted with any kind of frosting or covered with whipped cream and fresh strawberries.

Black Forest Cake

2 oz. kirsch

4 oz. grated
  unsweetened
  chocolate

3 c whipped cream,
  sweetened

3 c pitted cherries

2 9" chocolate
  cake layers

Temperature is a determining factor in assembling this cake. Refrigeration is imperative. The grated chocolate will melt when handled. The whipped cream will disintegrate if not kept chilled.

Either the $100 Cake or the Devil's Food Cake will work as the base for this delight. When the layers have thoroughly cooled, split them in half horizontally to form 4 delicately thin layers. Fill a spray bottle with kirsch. Spray the tops of all 4 layers with the kirsch.

Place the bottom layer on a cake plate. Spread with whipped cream about ½ inch thick. Cover the layer with cherries. Repeat the process until the top layer is placed. Cover the sides of the cake with the chocolate shavings, reserving a few for the center of the top of the cake. Place a ring of cherries round the edge of the top.

Refrigerate until serving time.

Blueberry Bran Muffins

Preheat oven to 350°
Makes 2 dozen

1¼ c boiling water
3 c bran
2 eggs
½ c oil
1 c honey
2 c buttermilk
2 c unbleached flour
½ t salt
½ t baking soda
2 c blueberries

In a mixing bowl, pour the boiling water over the bran. Wait a few minutes. Add the eggs and beat well. Next add the oil and the honey, again beating well. Sift the baking soda and salt into the flour. Add the buttermilk and flour alternately, stirring well after all are added. Mix the blueberries into the batter as little as possible to prevent the whole batter from turning blue.

Fill papered muffin tins ⅔ full of batter. Bake about 25 minutes, or until the centers of the muffins spring back after a soft touch.

Carrot Cake

Shena Waugh Sandler

Preheat oven to 350°
Makes 2 9" layers

½ c butter
1⅓ c granulated sugar
4 eggs
2½ c grated carrots
1 c pecan pieces
1 t salt
1 t baking soda
2 T cinnamon
2 c unbleached flour

Cream the butter, sugar, and eggs. Stir in the grated carrots and pecans.

Sift the flour before measuring. Stir the baking soda, salt, and cinnamon into the flour. Blend the dry ingredients into the batter. Pour the batter into pans that have been oiled and papered. Bake about 40 minutes or until the centers of the layers spring back after a gentle touch.

Corn Muffins

Cajun Style

Preheat oven to 400°

Makes 1 dozen

1½ c unbleached
   flour

1½ corn flour

3 T granulated sugar

1½ T baking powder

2 t salt

1 t cayenne pepper

1½ t black pepper

2 eggs

¼ c vegetable oil

1½ c buttermilk

¼ c diced red
   pepper

¼ c diced green
   pepper

¼ c diced onion

In a mixing bowl stir together the dry ingredients —flour, corn flour, sugar, baking powder, salt, cayenne and black pepper.

Add the diced vegetables and the wet ingredients to the dry. Mix until well blended.

Spoon the batter into well oiled muffin tins. Bake about 20 minutes. The muffins will be golden and crusty. Remove from pans while hot.

Devil's Food Cake

Barbara Sanford Smith

Preheat oven to 350°
Makes 2 9" layers

½ c water

3 unsweetened
   chocolate squares

½ c butter

¾ c granulated sugar

½ c brown sugar

2 eggs

1 t vanilla extract

⅔ c buttermilk

½ salt

1 t baking soda

2 c unbleached flour

Melt the chocolate squares in the water, being very careful to avoid scorching. Cream the butter, sugar, and eggs together until they are light. Stir in the vanilla and the chocolate mixture.

Sift, then measure the flour. Blend the salt and the baking soda into the flour. Alternately add the buttermilk and the dry ingredients to the batter. Pour the batter evenly into two 9" layer pans which have been oiled and lined with paper. Bake approximately 35 minutes or until the centers of the layers bounce back after a soft touch. This cake becomes dry and crumbly if baked too long.

Ebony Cake

Robert Schwartz

Preheat oven to 350°
Makes 2 8" layers

¾ c butter

1¾ c granulated sugar

3 oz. unsweetened chocolate

3 eggs

1½ t vanilla extract

¼ t almond extract

1½ c unbleached flour

1½ c walnuts, ground

1 T baking powder

½ t salt

⅜ c dark rum

⅜ c strongly brewed coffee

¾ c milk

Cream the butter, then add the sugar and eggs. Beat well. Melt the chocolate and blend in. Stir in the vanilla and almond extract.

Sift the flour, then measure. Add the salt and baking powder to the flour. If the nuts are ground in a blender, be sure to use a low speed to avoid reducing them to an oily paste. Stir the nuts into the dry mix.

Measure the coffee, rum, and milk together. Add the dry mix and the liquids to the batter alternately, beating well.

Pour into pans which have been oiled and papered. The tops of the papers should be oiled also. Bake for 35–45 minutes, until the center of the cake springs back when touched softly. This cake behaves strangely in the oven, and is very delicate. Remove from pans 5 minutes after taking from the oven. Wait 5 more minutes before removing the paper, to avoid uneven shrinkage.

To assemble: Fill with Mocha Butter Cream and frost with Chocolate Glaze.

Fairport Orange Cake

Barbara Sanford Smith

Preheat oven to 350°
Makes 2 9" layers

1 c granulated sugar
⅓ c butter
2 eggs
1 t vanilla
2 t grated orange rind
⅓ c chopped walnuts
1 c buttermilk
1 t baking soda
½ t salt
1¾ c unbleached
   flour

This is the easiest cake to make. Combine all ingredients in a bowl and mix until well blended.

Bake in two 9" layer pans which have been oiled and lined with paper. Baking time is approximately 40 minutes. The cake will pull away from the sides of the pan when done.

German Chocolate Cake

Frederick Becker

Preheat oven to 350°
Makes 2 9" layers

½ c water
3 oz. unsweetened
  chocolate
3 oz. white chocolate
½ c butter
¾ c granulated sugar
½ c brown sugar
2 eggs
1 t vanilla
1 t baking soda
½ t salt
2 c unbleached flour
⅔ c buttermilk

FILLING:
⅔ c cream
⅔ c brown sugar
2 egg yolks
⅓ c butter
1 t vanilla
¾ c coconut
⅔ c pecan pieces

Melt the chocolate in the water, in a small saucepan over low heat. Set aside.

Thoroughly cream the butter and sugars. Add the eggs and vanilla and beat until light and creamy. Stir the baking soda and salt into the flour. Alternately mix these dry ingredients and the buttermilk into the batter.

Pour the batter evenly into layer pans that have been lightly oiled and floured. Bake for 30 to 35 minutes, or until the centers of the layers spring back after a light touch. Cool on a wire rack.

To make the filling: Cook over medium heat and stirring occasionally, the cream, brown sugar, egg yolks, butter, and vanilla until they are thick. Add the coconut and pecans. Stir until the mixture is gooey. Allow the mixture to cool.

To assemble: After all the parts are cool, spread the bottom layer of cake with the filling. Add the top layer and spread the remaining filling.

$100 Cake

Gramma Degen

Preheat oven to 325°
Makes 2 9" layers

1 c brown sugar
1 c warm water
1 c mayonnaise
1 t vanilla extract
¼ c cocoa
2 t baking soda
½ t salt
2 c unbleached flour

Combine the water and brown sugar. Stir in the mayonnaise, vanilla, and cocoa.

Sift the flour before measuring. Stir the baking soda and salt into the flour. Work the dry ingredients into the batter, and beat well.

Pour the batter evenly into two 9" layer pans that have been oiled and lined with paper. Bake for 40 minutes or until the centers of the layers bounce back after a soft touch.

This dark, moist cake keeps well for days.

Orange Cake

Mom's Special

Preheat oven to 350°
Makes 2 9" layers

⅓ c butter
¾ c granulated sugar
2 eggs, separated
grated rind of
  1 orange
½ t lemon extract
½ t vanilla extract
¼ c orange juice
¼ c milk
2 t baking powder
¼ t salt
1¾ c unbleached
  flour

FILLING:
¾ c sugar
7 T flour
¼ t salt
2 egg yolks
grated rind of
  1 orange
⅜ c orange juice
1 T lemon juice

Cream the butter, then add the sugar and egg yolks, mixing thoroughly. Stir in the orange rind, lemon, and vanilla extract.

Sift the flour before measuring. Add to it the salt and the baking powder. Add the flour alternately with the milk, then add the orange juice. Beat well. Whip the egg whites, until stiff. Fold into the batter.

Bake in two 9" layer pans which have been oiled and lined with paper. Baking time should be about 30 minutes. The center of the cake should bounce back after a soft touch. Remove from pans when cooled. Split horizontally, spread with orange filling and stack.

Orange filling: In a saucepan mix the sugar, flour, and salt. Stir in the egg yolks and the grated orange rind. Slowly stir in the orange juice. Cook over a low heat, stirring constantly, until thick. Stir in the lemon juice. Cool to room temperature.

Poppy Seed Cake

The Irenean Hostage

Preheat oven to 350°
Makes 1 9" Tube Pan

1½ c granulated sugar
1½ c butter
3 eggs
1½ c milk
3 c unbleached flour
1 T baking powder
¼ t salt
⅜ c poppy seeds
1½ t vanilla extract

Thoroughly cream the butter and the sugar. Add the eggs, one at a time, then beat until the batter becomes light colored and fluffy.

Sift the flour, then measure. Add the salt and the baking powder to the flour and then sift again. Stir the poppy seeds into this dry mix.

Add the flour and the milk alternately to the mixture, and beat until smooth. Add the vanilla, and blend it into the batter.

Pour the batter into a tube pan which has been oiled and dusted with flour. Bake in a preheated oven for one hour. Remove from oven. After about 10 minutes remove the cake from the pan. Cool on a wire rack.

Pumpkin Cake

Preheat oven to 350°
Makes 2 9" layers

⅓ c butter
¾ c granulated sugar
3 eggs
1 t vanilla extract
1 c pumpkin, cooked
2 c unbleached flour
¼ t nutmeg
1 t cinnamon
1 t baking soda
¼ t salt
1 c milk

Thoroughly cream the butter and sugar. Add the eggs, one at a time, then the vanilla. Beat until light and fluffy. Add the pumpkin and mix until blended.

Measure out the flour by sifting it straight into a measuring cup. Stir into the flour the nutmeg, cinnamon, baking soda, and salt. Add these dry ingredients to the batter alternately with the milk.

Pour the batter into cake pans that have been lightly oiled, floured, and lined with paper. Place in the preheated oven. Bake for about 35 minutes or until the centers of the layers bounce back from a soft touch.

Sour Cream Pound Cake

Ward Bates

Preheat oven to 300°

Makes 1 10"
  tube cake

6 eggs, separated
1 c butter
2½ c granulated sugar
1 t vanilla extract
3 c unbleached flour,
  sifted
¼ t salt
¼ t baking soda
2 c sour cream

Beat the egg whites until stiff. Set aside.

Thoroughly cream the butter and sugar. Add the egg yolks, one at a time, mixing them in after each addition. Add the vanilla. Beat until light.

Mix the salt and baking soda into the flour. Add these dry ingredients to the batter alternately with the sour cream. Fold in the beaten egg whites.

Pour the batter into a tube pan that has been lightly oiled and floured. Bake for 1 hour. Allow to cool before removing from pan.

Strawberry Muffins

Inspiration at Zazou

Preheat oven to 400°
Makes 1 dozen

2 eggs
⅜ c vegetable oil
¾ c granulated sugar
2½ c unbleached
  flour
1½ T baking powder
½ t salt
¾ c slivered almonds
1½ c strawberries

Beat together the eggs, oil and sugar until they are creamy. In a separate bowl mix the baking powder, salt, and almonds into the flour. If the almonds are lightly toasted in the oven on a clean, dry pan, it enhances the flavor. This is not necessary, but a suggestion well worth the effort.

Enough fresh strawberries should be washed, hulled, and crushed to obtain 1½ cups of prepared fruit. If frozen, sweetened strawberries are utilized, then decrease the amount of sugar in the recipe by 2 tablespoons.

Add the dry ingredients alternately with the strawberries to the original mixture until all are evenly blended. Spoon the batter into an oiled muffin pan.

Bake in a preheated oven for approximately 20 minutes, or until the muffins appear golden brown. Remove from pan immediately after taking from the oven.

Sweet Potato Muffins

Preheat oven to 400°
Makes 1 dozen

2 eggs
2 c sweet potatoes
2 T soft butter
1 t vanilla extract
¾ c corn flour
⅔ c unbleached flour
½ c granulated sugar
2 T baking powder
1 t baking soda
½ t salt
¾ t nutmeg
1½ t cinnamon
½ c raisins
½ c chopped pecans
⅔ c buttermilk

Cook the sweet potatoes by steaming or boiling, until they are tender. After they are cooled, peel, mash, and measure them.

Whip the sweet potatoes with the eggs and the butter until light and fluffy. Add the vanilla. Stir.

Combine the dry ingredients in a separate bowl, stirring to ensure a smooth blend. Alternately add the dry ingredients and the buttermilk to the sweet potato batter, until mixed thoroughly.

Spoon the batter into an oiled muffin pan. Bake in a preheated oven until golden, which will take about 20 minutes. Remove from pan immediately after taking the muffins from the oven.

Upside Down Cake

Preheat oven to 325°
Makes a 9" cake

slices of pineapple or
  other fresh fruit
¾ c brown sugar
¼ c melted butter
2 eggs, separated
⅔ c granulated sugar
½ c fruit juice
1½ c unbleached
  flour, sifted
¼ t salt
1 t baking powder

whipped cream

When you preheat the oven, place a shallow pan of hot water in the oven on the lowest shelf. Lightly oil a round 9" pan and line the bottom with a circle of paper.

Carefully arrange the slices of pineapple, or apricot halves, or whatever fruit you select, in the bottom of the pan. The prettier side of the fruit should be down. Spread the brown sugar over the fruit and pour the melted butter over it.

Separate the eggs. Beat the whites until they form peaks and set aside.

Mix together the egg yolks and the granulated sugar until light and smooth. Stir in the fruit juice. Mix the salt and baking powder into the flour and gradually stir that into the batter until smooth.

Give the egg whites a stir to see if they have remained stiff. If some have reverted to their original condition, beat again until stiff. With a whisk or rubber spatula, fold the egg whites into the batter. Carefully pour the batter into the baking pan and place in oven.

Baking time is about an hour. Wait until the cake is cool before turning it onto a serving platter. Garnish with whipped cream.

White Chocolate Cake

Preheat oven to 350°
Makes 2 9" layers

¼ c water
3 oz. white chocolate
½ c butter
½ c granulated sugar
2 eggs
1 t vanilla
1 T white crème
   de cacao
2 c unbleached flour
½ t salt
1 t baking soda
⅔ c milk

Place the water and chocolate in a small pan and melt over low heat.

Thoroughly cream the butter and sugar. Add the eggs, one at a time, and then the vanilla and crème de cacao. Beat until light and fluffy. Add the white chocolate mixture and blend in.

Sift the flour straight into the measuring cup. Add the salt and baking soda to the flour. Add this dry mixture and the milk, alternately, to the batter.

Pour the batter into layer pans that have been lightly oiled, floured, and lined with paper. Bake for about 35 minutes or until golden on top and firm enough in the center to bounce back from a soft touch.

PIES &
TARTS

Basic Pastry

Preheat oven to 400°

**Makes a double
  9" crust**

2 c unbleached flour
1 t salt
⅓ c butter
⅓ c lard
5 T ice water

The less pastry is handled, the lighter it will be. The shortening should be cool. The water should be very cold.

I use butter for flavor and lard for tenderness. Sometimes I add fresh pressed garlic to a quiche crust or nutmeg to a sweet crust. Measure the flour and salt into a mixing bowl. Using a pastry blender or fork, cut in the shortening. After the shortening is in very small pieces add the water one tablespoon at a time, until the dough holds together.

Roll on a pastry cloth or waxed paper. Avoid handling. Pie shells should have a few strategically placed fork marks to prevent huge bubbles.

To make tart shells: Roll out a large portion of dough, cut into 5" squares, mould into cupcake pans. Puncture the bottoms of the shells with a fork.

Bake until golden, or about 20 minutes.

Armadillos' Ecstasies

Madeleine McCarthy

Fills 1 dozen tarts

16 oz. cream cheese
1 medium banana
1 medium ripe
  avocado
1 T honey
1 T lemon juice
1 c toasted cashews

Whip the cream cheese until light and smooth. Add the banana and avocado, and whip until smooth. Next, add the honey and lemon juice and beat only until blended.

Fill the tart shells and top with toasted cashews. Refrigerate.

Armadillos have walked all the way from Texas for one of these.

Banana Cream Pie

Melinda J. Gleason

Makes 1 9" pie

⅓ c granulated sugar
3 T cornstarch
¼ t salt
1½ c milk
2 egg yolks, beaten
2 T butter
2 t vanilla extract
2 egg whites, beaten
¼ c granulated sugar

2 bananas
1 c whipping cream
2 T powdered sugar
½ t vanilla extract
1 baked 9" pie shell

Combine in a saucepan ⅓ c sugar, cornstarch, and salt. Gradually stir in the milk, then the egg yolks. Cook until thick.

Remove from heat before stirring in the butter and vanilla. Cool at room temperature.

Beat the egg whites until they form soft peaks. Add ¼ c sugar and continue to beat until stiff peaks form. Fold this mixture carefully into the egg yolk mixture.

Layer the sliced bananas and the custard into a cooked 9" pie shell. Refrigerate until serving. Top with sweetened whipped cream.

Chocolate Pecan Bourbon Pie

Esther Carpenter

Preheat oven to 400°
Makes 1 9" pie

4 eggs
3 T melted butter
⅓ c granulated sugar
⅔ c brown sugar
⅓ c corn syrup
3 T maple syrup
1 oz. bourbon
1 t vanilla extract
1 c pecan halves
⅔ c chocolate chips

1 uncooked 9" pie
shell

Beat the eggs. Pour in the melted butter, and continue to beat until well blended. Add the granulated sugar and incorporate into a smooth mixture. Add the brown sugar and blend until all the lumps disappear. Stir in the corn syrup, maple syrup, bourbon, and vanilla.

Set this mixture aside for a moment while you line an uncooked pie shell with the chocolate chips. Pour in the filling mixture. Place the pecan halves neatly to cover the top of the mixture.

Place the pie in the oven, close the door, and immediately lower the temperature to 275°. Cooking time is at least an hour. When the filling has set at the center, the pie is done.

Buttermilk Custard

Ira Long, Jr.

Preheat oven to 300°
Makes 1 9" pie

1 T butter
1 c granulated sugar
2 eggs
1 t vanilla extract
1 pinch nutmeg
2 T flour
½ t baking powder
½ t baking soda
1 c buttermilk

uncooked 9" pie shell

Cream the butter and sugar. Add the eggs, vanilla, nutmeg, flour, and baking powder. With a fork stir the baking soda into the buttermilk, then add this to the batter. Pour into an uncooked 9" pie shell. Sprinkle with freshly grated nutmeg. Bake until set at the center, about 45 minutes.

Chocolate Cream Tarts

Anne E. Degen

Fills 1 dozen tarts

1½ c whipping cream
3 T cocoa
6 T powdered sugar
1 c chocolate chips

Whip the cream until it forms soft peaks. Sift in the cocoa and powdered sugar. Whip a minute more. Mound into baked tart shells. Top with a few chocolate chips. Chill until serving.

Cranberry Apple Pie

Preheat oven to 400°
Makes 1 9" pie

2 c raw cranberries
1 c water
2 c sliced apples
1 c granulated sugar
1 t cinnamon
4 T cornstarch
1 t vanilla extract

1 uncooked 9" pie shell with additional pie dough for latticed top
cinnamon sugar

Cook the cranberries with the water in a covered saucepan, until the cranberry skins pop. Add the sliced apples and cook for a couple of minutes more. Remove from heat.

Stir in the sugar, cinnamon, cornstarch, and vanilla. Pour into the uncooked pie shell. Place the lattice strips on the top of the pie filing. Sprinkle with cinnamon sugar.

Bake in the 400° oven for 10 minutes. Reduce the oven temperature to 300° and continue to bake until the pie bubbles in the center, then remove from oven. This pie is best when served warm.

Key Lime Pie

Jon Kronenberg

Makes 1 9" pie

1 envelope unflavored
 gelatin
¼ c water
½ c granulated sugar
¼ t salt
½ c lime juice
4 eggs, separated
¼ c granulated sugar

1 c whipping cream
2 T powdered sugar
1 baked 9" pie shell

Dissolve the gelatin in water and set aside. Measure the ½ c sugar and the salt into a saucepan. Gradually stir in the lime juice. Stir in the egg yolks, which have been well beaten. While stirring, cook until thick. Remove from heat and stir in the gelatin. Cool to room temperature. Whip the egg whites until they form soft peaks. Gradually add the ¼ cup of sugar and continue to whip until stiff. Fold the whites into the yolk mixture. Pour into a cooked pie shell. Refrigerate. Top with whipped cream before serving.

Lemon Meringue

Makes 1 9" pie

FILLING:

¼ c lemon juice

1 t finely grated
lemon peel

½ c granulated sugar

3 T cornstarch

¼ t salt

1 c water

3 egg yolks

1 T butter

MERINGUE:

3 egg whites, at room
temperature

⅛ t cream of tartar

2 T granulated sugar

1 baked 9" pie shell

Prepare the lemon juice and peel. Fill the bottom of a double boiler with water, cover, and place on heat.

In the top of the double boiler combine the dry ingredients: granulated sugar, cornstarch, and salt. Gradually add water, stirring to make sure no lumps form. Whisk in the egg yolks.

Place over the bottom of the double boiler and stir until thickened. Remove from heat.

Stir in the butter, lemon juice, and peel. Pour into the cooked, cooled pie shell. Refrigerate without disturbing until thoroughly chilled.

Before starting to make the meringue, turn on the oven to 400°. Beat the egg whites with the cream of tartar and sugar until smooth, shiny, and stiff. Cover the top of the pie with the meringue, using a spatula or a pastry tube. Replace in the oven for just a couple of minutes, until the tips of the meringue brown. (If heated too long, the meringue will shrink.) Remove from oven and serve or return to refrigerator.

Peach Daiquiri Pie

The customers of Magazine Cuisine

Makes 1 9" pie

1 T unflavored gelatin
¼ c water
4 eggs, separated
½ c granulated sugar,
2 T fresh lime juice
3 c fresh peaches,
   puréed
¼ c rum

1 9" baked pie
   shell
whipped cream
8 slices lime

Dissolve the gelatin in the water and set aside. Beat the egg whites with ¼ cup of sugar until they form stiff peaks. Set aside.

Put the remaining sugar into a saucepan. Stir in the lime juice. Add the egg yolks, one at a time, stirring until smooth after each addition. Add the pureed peaches. Place over heat and stir constantly until thick. Remove from heat. Add the rum and the gelatin mix. Fold in the beaten egg whites.

Pour into the pie shell and chill undisturbed for at least 1 hour. Before serving, top with whipped cream and garnish each piece with a lime slice.

Peanut Butter Pie

Preheat oven to 375°
Makes 1 9" pie

CRUST:
3 T oil
¼ c peanut butter
¾ c granulated sugar
1 egg yolk
½ t vanilla extract
½ t baking powder
1 c unbleached flour

FILLING:
4 eggs, separated
4 T granulated sugar
1 c granulated sugar
6 T cornstarch
2½ c heavy cream
½ c peanut butter
1⅓ T vanilla extract

whipped cream
semi-sweet chocolate
  shavings

To make the crust: Thoroughly cream the oil, peanut butter, sugar, egg yolk, and vanilla. Stir the baking powder into the flour. Add the dry mix and blend completely. Chill this dough for ½ hour. Press the dough into the pie pan. Make several fork punctures in the bottom. Bake for about 10 minutes or until golden. Allow to cool before filling.

To make the filling: Beat the egg whites with the 4 T of sugar until they form soft peaks. Set aside.

Combine, in a saucepan, the cup of sugar with the cornstarch. Add enough of the cream to make a smooth, liquid mixture. Stir in the egg yolks, until evenly blended. Add the rest of the cream, the peanut butter, and the vanilla. The peanut butter will blend in smoothly during the cooking process. Cook this mixture, stirring constantly until thick. Remove from heat. Fold in the egg whites.

To assemble: Cover the bottom of the crust with chocolate shavings. Add the filling. Sprinkle the top of the filling with more chocolate shavings. Using a pastry tube, pipe the whipped cream on top and sprinkle with even more chocolate shavings. Chill before serving.

Pecan Pie

Preheat oven to 400°
Makes 1 9" pie

3 eggs
2 T melted butter
½ c brown sugar
1 t vanilla extract
1 c light corn sryup
1 c pecans

1 9" uncooked pie
shell

Beat the eggs. Pour in the melted butter, and continue beating until the color is noticeably lighter. Sprinkle in the brown sugar while the beating continues. Add the vanilla and corn syrup. Blend until smooth. Pour into an uncooked 9" pastry shell. Cover the top with pecans.

Bake at 400° for 10 minutes. Lower the oven temperature to 350° and bake until set up in the center, approximately 25 minutes more.

Strawberry Rhubarb Tarts

Makes 1 dozen

4 c fresh rhubarb
⅔ c water
½ c honey
3 T cornstarch
1 t vanilla extract
2 c fresh strawberries, sliced

Wash the rhubarb and cut into two inch pieces. Place in a covered saucepan with water and cook until softened, about 15 minutes. Combine the honey, cornstarch, and vanilla into a smooth mixture. Add these to the rhubarb, and continue to cook, stirring constantly. When the rhubarb has split into fibers, and the mixture has thickened, remove from heat. Stir in the strawberries, which have been washed and sliced. Pour into baked tart shells and refrigerate until served.

Pumpkin Pie

Preheat oven to 400°
Makes 1 9" pie

1½ c pumpkin pulp
⅔ c brown sugar
½ t cinnamon
¼ t ginger
¼ t nutmeg
2 eggs
1 c whipping cream
½ c bourbon
3 T pecan pieces

1 9" uncooked pie
  shell

Bake a pastry shell 5 minutes. Reduce oven temperature to 350°

Blend the pumpkin with the brown sugar, spices, and eggs. Stir in the bourbon. Whip the cream until peaked. Fold into the pumpkin mix. Ladle into the pastry shell. Sprinkle the top with pecans.

Bake 25 or 30 minutes, or until the center has set.

Sweet Potato Pie

Preheat oven to 400°
Makes 1 9" pie

1½ c cooked sweet
  potatoes
3 eggs
1 c heavy cream
¾ c brown sugar
1 t cinnamon
½ t nutmeg
1 t vanilla extract
1 T rum

1 uncooked 9" pie
  shell
whipped cream
toasted pecans

Beat the cooked sweet potatoes until smooth and creamy. Add the eggs, cream, and brown sugar and beat until light. Blend in the cinnamon, nutmeg, vanilla, and rum.

Pour this filling into the uncooked pie shell and bake in the preheated oven for 10 minutes. Reduce the heat to 325° and continue to bake until golden. Remove from the oven and cool.

Before serving, top with the whipped cream and garnish with toasted pecans.

FROSTINGS, GLAZES, & ICINGS

Mocha Butter Cream

1 c butter

4 T strong-brewed
  coffee

2 c powdered sugar

Whip the butter until light and creamy. Add the coffee and the powdered sugar at the same time, and beat until smooth.

Orange Frosting

6 T butter

juice of 1 orange

grated rind of
  1 orange

3 c powdered sugar

Whip the butter until soft. Then add all other ingredients and beat until of spreading consistency.

Raspberry Icing
(for your Valentines)

¼ c raspberry juice,
  fresh or frozen

¼ c butter

1 c powdered sugar

Whip the butter until light. Add the juice and sugar at the same time. Beat until smooth and spreadable.

Sweet Bread Glaze I

4 T lemon juice

2 c powdered sugar

Beat until smooth.

Sweet Bread Glaze II

¼ c milk
1 t vanilla extract
2 c powdered sugar

Whip together until light and smooth.

Sweet E. Bun Glaze

8 oz. cream cheese
⅔ c honey
½ t vanilla extract

Cream the cream cheese until soft and smooth.
Gradually add the honey, being sure to avoid
lumps. Add the vanilla and whip until light.

Chocolate Glaze

1 c semi-sweet
  chocolate chips
3 T dark rum
12 T unsalted butter

Melt the chocolate in the rum, being careful not to
scorch. Stir in the butter 1 T at a time.
Beat over cold water to spreading consistency.

Chocolate Frosting

⅔ c melted butter
⅔ c cocoa
⅔ c milk
2 t vanilla extract
6 c powdered sugar

Whip together all ingredients until smooth,
and of spreading consistency,

Brandy Orange Icing

⅓ c butter
¼ c cream cheese
3 T brandy
3 T orange juice
1 T grated orange
  rind
3 c powdered sugar

Whip together all ingredients until smooth, and of spreading consistency,

Cream Cheese Icing

½ c butter
8 oz. cream cheese
4 t vanilla extract
¼ t lemon juice
4 c powdered sugar

Beginning with the butter and cream cheese, beat together all ingredients until smooth.

Danish Glaze

¾ c water
1 T lemon juice
1 t vanilla extract
2 c powdered sugar

Blend all of the ingredients until smooth.

Lebkuchen Glaze

3 T hot water
½ t vanilla extract
1 t lemon juice
1½ c powdered sugar

Beat all the ingredients until smooth.